Confused and Abused

Fauneil Fremont

The Reading Glass Books
1-888-420-3050
www.readingglassbooks.com
production@readingglassbooks.com

Dedication page:

To

Those who have experienced

physical, emotional, and/or financial abuse

Table of Contents

Chapter I: Brioletta Martin 1

Chapter II: Covid Strikes!........................ 6

Chapter III: Richie Campianno........................ 12

Chapter IV: Houston 21

Chapter V: Business Deals........................ 28

Chapter VI: How Could He? 36

Chapter VII: Separation 42

Chapter VIII: Relationship Rekindled?.............. 49

Chapter IX: Paris........................ 55

Chapter X: In the SUV 62

Chapter XI: Fear 74

Chapter XII: Be Mine 84

Chapter XIII: Living with Jena........................ 92

Chapter XIV: Decisions and Consequences....... 98

Chapter XV: Return to San Antonio 103

Chapter XVI: Escape 116

Chapter XVII: Finding a Way 124

Chapter XVIII: Determination........................ 133

Chapter XIX: Wounded 141

Chapter XX: What about Richie? 151

Chapter XXI: Confused 157

Chapter XXII: The Healing of Brio 162

Chapter XXIII: Seeking Justice....................... 166

Preface by the Author

My personal experiences and my study of victims who are targeted for abuse led me to write the story of Brio and Richie. The names of the characters are fictional, but the narrative is primarily factual. As I tell the story, I describe Paris and its environs and the Midwest and Southwest of the United States, taking the reader on journeys that are risky and thought-provoking.

I portray Brio, the main character, as a widow who is looking for a new location that will lead her to fulfillment in her life. When she meets Richie, she thinks she has found it.

Chapter I

Brioletta Martin

Brioletta (Brio) was a woman of determination. She had been determined to make a success of her marriage to Benjamin (Ben), an Englishman, whose accent and background had intrigued her. Friends described their marriage as a success. They both had rewarding careers, Ben as a mathematician, and Brio as a teacher and musician. Ben had been a devoted and affectionate father to Lily, their only child. For the majority of their years together, Ben and Brio lived in California. Shortly after they moved to Santa Fe, New Mexico, Ben was diagnosed with prostate and bone cancer, and Brio became his nurse and caregiver. When he died, she lived for a year in a cocoon of widowhood, tying up the loose ends of Ben's life. However, after a year, she was determined to break out of the past and test her wings for a new location and a new life.

Where to go? On her computer, she searched for a city that would be ideal: a place large enough to have interesting sights and activities, located in a warm climate, and offering good health care and affordable housing. San Antonio, Texas seemed to have everything she was looking for. Her first step in preparing to move was to contact a realtor in Santa Fe to draw up a listing of her property: a one-story pueblo-styled house in the Eldorado section; three bedrooms, two baths, kitchen, living/dining room, laundry room, two-car garage on two acres of native terrain with cacti, desert brush, and cedar trees and three beautifully landscaped walled gardens with brick patio and stone pathways.

Next, she contacted Michelle, a realtor in San Antonio, to show her properties during a weekend trip there. The weather was hot and humid when Brio arrived in late August, but Michelle countered that with a cool, elegant room at Hotel Emma in the Pearl District of San Antonio. Brio had time to see a number of residences in different areas, to visit the shops and restaurants near the hotel, and to walk along the scenic riverbank. Michelle enumerated all of the attractions that San Antonio offered: the historic Alamo, two art museums, several missions, a botanical garden, parks, and the Tower of America.

By the end of the weekend, Brio had purchased a condo in the Alamo Heights area, which had once been a fashionable suburb for the wealthy and now had a mixture of stately, older homes and apartment and condo buildings. Shops, restaurants, offices, and churches were nearby, and the condo was centrally located in San Antonio, with easy access to the freeways. On the plane back to Santa Fe, Brio felt excited. San Antonio would be an ideal spot to live!

Brio put her house up for sale and got ready for the move. She divided her belongings into three lots: one to send to Lily in California, one to move to Texas, and the rest to donate to charity or to dispose of.

She kept most of her antiques, baby grand piano, artworks, and collectibles. She realized that her condo might look like a lived-in museum, but each piece was connected to a memory, which she was not ready to lose. With her Santa Fe residence in the hands of the realtor, Brio said goodbye to special friends and set out in the car with her 18-year-old cat, Mickey. (The moving van would meet her at the condo three days later.) Having had the experience of a three-week car trip with Brio and Ben throughout the Midwest, Mickey was a seasoned traveler. Brio had put a comfortable pillow for him on the front seat next to her, but he preferred her lap. From time to time, he stretched up to look at the passing scenery: at first, the desert, then the derricks pumping up and down in the oilfields, the green fields of corn and cattle in the pastures on the second day, and as San Antonio grew closer, the Hill Country of Texas, giving way to flatter land near the city.

As she approached the outskirts of San Antonio, the traffic became increasingly heavy, and she realized that adjusting to the highway system in the city would not be easy. Two ring roads, called loops, encircled the city, and the interstate and state highways radiated from the center outward to the suburbs. The robot in the GPS system was doing its best to guide Brio, but because of her nervousness and unfamiliarity with the pronunciation of the streets that she whizzed by, she kept taking wrong exits and needed to be rerouted. When she finally reached her condo in Alamo Heights, she was exhausted; she carried only the blankets, pillows, and Mickey's supplies into the kitchen. After attending to his food, water, and sandbox, she arranged a blanket and a pillow on the floor as a temporary bed. Mickey settled next to her and fell asleep in the crook of her legs.

Brio's goal was to be settled by Christmastime. Finding a church home was high on her "to-do" list. After attending a Methodist, a Lutheran, and three Episcopal churches, she chose St. Luke's Episcopal in Alamo Heights, located near the Quarry Shopping Center, in a woody, hilly area dotted with numerous large oak trees. The church sat atop a hill. As Brio drove up the winding gravel path to the parking lot for the morning service, the steeple of the church spire seemed to say, "Leave the world behind." Inside the church, the beauty of the nave inspired her to do just that. Large stained-glass windows reached twenty feet upward to the vaulted ceiling. As the service began, organ and choral music filled the air, and she relaxed into serenity. At the coffee hour following the service, Brio met a number of parishioners: a local actor, a couple who were planning a trip abroad, and a member of the choir. Each attempted to help her feel at home.

Driving to church, she had passed the Quarry Shopping Center, where she now stopped at Alexander's for lunch. Before heading back to the condo, she acquainted herself with the center, discovering future shopping and entertainment spots: a clothing store, two grocery stores, a salon, a gym, and a movie theater. In the next few weeks, she began to frequent places on Broadway, a major street within easy walking distance of her condo, including Broadway Pharmacy, Bird Bakery, Daily Bread, Panera, and a large HEB supermarket. She also found nearby a primary care physician who had a similar background to hers. Both had been raised in Nebraska and had attended the University of Nebraska.

By Christmastime, Brio had achieved her goal, to be settled in San Antonio. She was looking forward to 2020 and the New Year!

Chapter II

Covid Strikes!

On January 23rd, when Brio awoke and looked at the time and date on her cell phone, she thought, *Oh! It's Dad's birthday; I have to call him today.* A moment later, she remembered that he had passed on several years ago. She got up, but continued to feel groggy as she dressed for the day. She walked down to the kitchen, plugged in the coffee maker, selected puffed rice for breakfast, and fed Mickey.

"Let's go out on the deck," she said to Mickey. "It looks nice out – sun's shining, no wind today."

Mickey jumped up on top of the low surrounding wall to examine the garden below before settling down to watch Brio as she sipped her coffee and took an occasional bite of her cereal.

Her hands were a bit shaky, and she dribbled her cereal and then her coffee down her sweater.

Shoot, be careful, you klutz, she warned herself. Taking another spoonful, she dribbled again. She decided that it was too flavorless to pursue. She set it down for Mickey, who gave it one sniff and apparently agreed with her.

Brio shivered. "It's chilly out here, Mickey. Let's go inside." She took a last swallow of her coffee. *Hm, sore throat starting.* "Let's go upstairs, Mickey, and crawl into bed to get warm." Several hours later, she awoke to the landline ringing. *Let the answering machine take the message,* she told herself. When the message stopped, a buzzing sound continued inside her ears. Brio reached for her cell phone to check the time and the date, but she had trouble focusing. Her dizziness was increasing, her sore throat was worsening, her body temperature was alternating between chills and fever, and a headache was starting at the back of her head. She stumbled to the bathroom, took two Excedrin, urinated, and stumbled back to bed. "Mickey," she called. "Come back to bed." Mickey willingly climbed under the covers and snuggled next to her for his morning nap.

When Brio awoke, it was dark. *It can't be night already,* she thought, *Mickey must be hungry.* When she arose, he jumped down from the bed and followed her down the stairs and into the kitchen. Brio fed him a small can of Chicken Delight and then lifted the carton of dry food from the cabinet to refill his bowl. Her hands shook so uncontrollably that she spilled half of it onto the floor. *Damn, you klutz,* she scolded herself again.

Leaving Mickey to finish eating, she began climbing the stairs, her legs feeling wobbly and weak. Her arms seemed to have lost their strength, too. She was beginning to shiver and shake again. She piled several blankets from the closet onto her bed before attempting to turn off the table lamp at her bedside. Finding the light switch too stiff to turn, she gave up and fell into bed. (It was fortunate that Brio had left the lamp on because several times during the night, she had to pile on more blankets and then coats to keep from "freezing."

In the morning, she was drenched in sweat; her body, pajamas, and bedclothes were all damp. Her chills had been replaced with extreme aches and exhaustion. She put on fresh pajamas, toddled over to the spare bedroom, pulled back the covers, and called to Mickey. "Come on! I'm in **here.**"

Several days later, Brio crawled out of bed. Gone were the fever and chills, loss of senses, sore throat, headache, and dizziness. Instead, she felt like an old woman with atrophied muscles and a loss of energy. Going up and down stairs became an athletic challenge. Each step needed to be conquered by her right foot and then her left, aided by her right arm muscle on the railing. The twenty stairs between the two stories now took five or more minutes instead of one. Brio realized that she had been, and still was, very ill. She had had no ordinary case of the flu. She decided that she needed to see her doctor.

Dr. Stellman chided her for not coming in sooner. Like thousands of patients, she had been the victim of an epidemic hitting the nation. When Brio described her fatigue and loss of muscle strength, he ordered bed rest and home health care for her.

It took Brio three months to lose the "old lady" feeling. She had regressed into her cocoon and needed time to regain the strength to crawl out of it.

In the meantime, society in general began shutting down. Masks were now mandatory for entrance into all buildings. People in lines were required to stand six feet apart. Businesses had either closed or were operating by customer pick-up or online. Fewer cars were on the roads because many employees were working from home. Communal worship services had been replaced with streaming services. Teachers and students were working together online instead of in classrooms. Doctors were consulting with patients by virtual online visits. Many pharmacies and supermarkets were delivering goods to help to prevent the spread of germs.

Brio ventured out one sunny day in May to go to the supermarket.She planned to stop first at Panera for a croissant and coffee. When she pulled into the parking lot, the area looked deserted. The restaurant was closed and a notice had been posted on the door, giving instructions for Take-out. That meant eating and drinking in the car or driving home with containers. *What a bummer*, she said to herself. *I might as well be a hermit!*

She skipped the snack and drove to the parking lot in front of HEB. As she entered the store, an employee stood guard by the grocery carts to keep anyone unmasked from entering. Inside the store, the floor was marked with instructions for waiting to be served or to be checked out. Although the aisles were filled with masked customers, many shelves were empty. One of the items sold out was toilet paper. However, Brio noticed some hoarders whose carts were filled with two or more large packages of toilet rolls. Some of Brio's favorite brands of food, like Cornflakes, were gone. Brio felt lucky when she grabbed the last container of 2% milk. On the way to check-out, she looked for bottled water, but the shelves were empty. "Empty!" said Brio to the lady behind her, who responded only with a slight shake of her head.

"Why are the shelves so empty?" Brio asked the employee at the check-out stand.

"Lack of employees throughout the nation – manufacturers, truckers, shippers – you name it. We're short-handed here."

"I better start watching the news more," responded Brio.

At home, Brio began watching a number of different stations. She gained very little information about the nature of Covid because scientists had conflicting views about its source or treatment. However, she learned a lot about social situations throughout the nation. Each state was under firm management by the governor and the bureaucrats. A Democratic governor generally handled the health issues by controlling society with rules and regulations, including schools, churches, and businesses. A Republican governor tended to be more lenient, allowing individual organizations to make their own decisions.

The blame game was in full force. Republicans accused Democrats of taking measures that brought the U.S. economy to the brink of collapse. Democrats accused Republicans of failing to take enough measures to stop the spread of Covid. The leading bureaucrat, a doctor/politician, became the czar of health in the U.S. Unfortunately, he disagreed with many doctors on how to treat Covid. Some patients got little care or received it too late. Many patients died alone, their loved ones restricted from being at their bedside. The death toll rose for the elderly and for those who had serious health issues.

Brio was no different from millions of senior citizens. She lived in isolation. The grocery store and pharmacy were open to her, **if** she wore a mask, but all communal activities were on hold. Communication was mainly by phone or internet. Since Brio was new to San Antonio, her major sources of feeling alive were the weekly phone calls from Lily in California and from Maggie in Nebraska. These helped her temporarily feel less lonely.

Chapter III
Richie Campianno

In July of 2020, Brio's computer was hacked into. She had lost contact with the outside world, and she felt even more isolated. Because she couldn't search for help on a non-functioning computer, she called her family in California. Melanie, her granddaughter, agreed to help. She researched computer technology businesses online in San Antonio and then called Brio with several names and phone numbers, each with good ratings by customers.

On her landline, Brio called My Computer Security. Miguel, a technician, agreed to come to her condo, even though most employees were not making house calls. When he came, he was unable to solve the problem. He called his boss for help and left. At 9:00 p.m. there was a knock on the door. Brio opened to a man who introduced himself as Richie Campianno, the Director of My Computer Technology. Brio greeted him and then led him upstairs to the computer in the office. As she followed him up the stairs, she noticed that he was of medium height, with square shoulders and a muscular build.

While he worked at the computer, Brio seated herself on a nearby low stool that was close to the computer. It did not take him long to discover that the hacking had been extensive. He turned the computer chair around to face Brio and asked her questions, to ascertain her knowledge of the software on her computer. Determining that her knowledge was very little, he drew a quick diagram on a sheet of paper and kneeled on the floor to explain it to her. As he talked, he looked at her to verify that she was understanding it. Brio noticed that he was a mature man with a serious demeanor.

"Well, Ma'am, he said, "it looks like your Dell has been badly damaged by the hacker."

"How badly? Can it be repaired?"

"I would have to study it to determine if the mother board has been damaged. If so, it is not repairable."

"So, you need to take the computer apart?"

"Yes, I can do that at the office where I have the tools I need. Would that be O.K. with you?"

"Yes, but I hope it won't take too long. I'm behind in my emails."

"You seem like an intelligent woman. It won't take you long to catch up."

"Why do you say *intelligent*?"

"From your questions."

"Well, you've been helpful, Mr. Campianno."

"And you've been warm and friendly." He looked around at the furnishings in the room. "It's like a touch of home here," he added.

"Home? Where's home for you?"

"Italy. Your blue eyes remind me of my grandmother and your nose of my mother."

He smiled impishly and pointed to his nose. Brio changed the subject. "Mr. Campianno, do you think the hacker could be identified? I was suspicious when I called Dell for help and got a man with a broad Indian accent."

"That probably was a hacker pretending to be from Dell. You know, cyber security is part of our business. I'll see if I can trace the location." He handed Brio his business card, disconnected the computer, and carried it downstairs.

"I'll contact you by phone within the week. Thank you, Ma'am."

A week later, Richie called Brio to inform her that the motherboard had been badly damaged and was not repairable. The hacker had come from India, and the FBI had been informed because it was a cyber security matter.

"Would you like me to set you up with another computer?" asked Richie.

"Yes. What do you recommend?"

"An MSI, made in Japan. Excellent hardware. Good speed. A bit expensive, though."

"I'm not worried about the expense, but can you transfer my information from the Dell?"

"Yes, but I recommend that we not transfer any communication with Dell since that led to the hacking. If you like, I'll put on new software that you will need, do the transfer, and organize your files onto the desktop."

"Yes. Please do, and call me if you have questions. Also, will you have the Dell destroyed?"

"Absolutely. I'll call you when the task is completed and set up a time for me to install the MSI."

As Brio reflected on the last two weeks of being again cut off from the outside world, she remembered the relief she had felt when her granddaughter had put her in touch with a reputable company. She would be better able now to function in this Covid-riddled society. She knew where to go for computer help. Mr. Campianno seemed knowledgeable. And he was friendly and good-looking, as well.

Two weeks later, Richie returned with a new MSI computer and the necessary power cord and internet connecter needed for installation. As he left, he said that he would stop by when he was in the area, to see how she was getting along. When Brio closed the door, she wondered about his wanting to stop by. He could just call. *Oh, heck,* she thought, *he's nice, he's company, he's been helpful; just go along with it."*

A week later, Richie knocked on her door and asked how the equipment was behaving and how she was feeling. Brio answered, "Much better, now that I have a computer that is working. I don't feel so cooped up."

"You look like you're feeling better. Quite good, actually." He smiled broadly.

"Thanks. It's been a difficult time with Covid." She was happy to have a "live" person to communicate with and invited him in for coffee. As they sat sipping their coffee in the kitchen, they exchanged information about their professional backgrounds. Brio described herself as a perennial student, earning degrees in education, English, and music. She had had two careers, first as an English teacher and then as a church pipe organist. Richie revealed that he had had his basic schooling abroad and had graduated from an Italian college before employment with the United Nations in Geneva, Switzerland. After three years, he had emigrated to the U.S., where he was trained in cyber security and technology in Washington, D.C.

"Very impressive," said Brio when he paused.

"You're impressive, Mrs. Martin. May I call you by your first name?"

"Sure. It's Brio."

"Brio! That's very musical."

"Yes," responded Brio. "It's actually a musical term, meaning with *vivacity* or with *fire and energy*."

"That suits you," he responded. "I'd like to get to know you better, Brio. I would ask you out, but everything is closed, except our homes"

"I don't really know much about you," said Brio.

"I can change that. Aren't you tired of being alone and cooped up?"

"Yes," answered Brio. "So, would you like to come for dinner on the 18th?"

Brio had not had company for dinner since moving to San Antonio. She decided to fix something simple: roast beef, potatoes, carrots and green beans, a tossed salad, and apple pie for dessert – a very American menu. She would serve a red wine with the beef.

The day of the dinner, she set two place settings at a small table in the living room with her Castleton China, Francis I Reed and Barton silverware, and crystal goblets. The flowers she gathered from the garden were yellow roses, which complemented the chinaware pattern. She decided against candles. *Too suggestive of romance. Keep it friendly*, she told herself. While the beef was roasting, she dressed conservatively for the evening in a pink silk blouse, tailored black skirt, and black low-heeled pumps. Richie arrived in a gray dress shirt, gray woolen trousers, and black loafers. He handed Brio a dozen white roses.

"For you, Brio." He sniffed. "Mm, it smells like roast beef."

"Yes, it's ready. Please be seated while I bring the Cabernet and the salad," she said.

During the dinner, Richie seemed a little cool. Brio wondered if he felt uncomfortable with the formal table setting and the antique furniture. However, when Mickey jumped up onto his lap, Richie responded with warmth. Coffee outdoors on the deck followed, with Mickey joining them.

"I'm glad you like cats," commented Brio.

"I do. I have two of my own, both Russian blues."

"Oh, that's a beautiful breed. What are their names?"

"Basha and Maya."

"Is Basha an Italian name?"

"No, it's Lebanese. My mother is Lebanese; my father is Italian."

"Ah, that explains your tan skin and brown eyes." Richie pointed to his eyes.

"How about my long, curved eyelashes?"

"Pretty, and you don't need mascara."

"How about my nose?"

"How about a change of topic?"

"How about inviting me to stay, Brio?"

"How about the word *no?*"

"How about the word *please?*"

"How about the word *goodnight?*"

When Brio escorted him to the entrance hall, she held the door open for him. He reached for her and kissed her. She responded with a smile and a warm "Goodnight."

Richie wasted no time. A few days later, he dropped by for coffee on the deck. He wanted it strong and black. While they sipped their coffee, he smoked three cigarettes.

"You seem to smoke a lot," observed Brio. "How old were you when you started?"

"Eleven. My uncle addicted me. Whenever he came, we went out to the toolshed for a smoke."

"Didn't your parents know you were smoking?"

"No, not until several years later. Strong mints, from my uncle, were a good camouflage."

"You know, the younger you are when you begin smoking, the more difficult it is to give up."

"I know. I've tried more than once." He reached for another cigarette from the packet in his pocket.

"One for the road," he said as he led the way to the front door. "By the way, I'm going to Houston this weekend on business. Want to go with me, Brio?"

"I don't know. Saturday is my birthday."

"Good. Let's combine business with celebration!"

Chapter IV

Houston

Richie called for Brio on Saturday in his vintage black Mercedes sedan. Brio commented on its beautiful interior: black leather seats, wood dashboard, and lush carpets. He headed for Highway 10 East, which led to Houston.

"How far is it?" asked Brio when they were underway.

"About 200 miles, a three-or-four-hour drive, depending upon the traffic. There's a map in the pocket of your door if you want to follow our route." Brio found Highway 10 on the map and read the names of towns along the way: "Seguin, Luling, Flatonia, Schulenberg, Columbus, Katy, Houston. Hm, you've marked the town, Luling, with the word, Buc-ee's. Sounds like the name of a ranch."

"No, but Buc-ee's probably gets their beef from a nearby ranch. It's a huge petrol station with a take-out restaurant, where I usually stop to get a barbequed brisket sandwich. It's the best!"

"Okay, chef, what makes it the best?"

"They take a cut of beef called brisket and rub it with spices, then wrap it in foil, and smoke it for eight to twelve hours, then unwrap it and douse it with their special barbeque sauce, rewrap it, and slow-cook it for about four hours longer. The time depends upon the size of the brisket."

Richie stopped at Buc-ee's and picked up two barbequed brisket sandwiches for lunch. On the way from Luling to Houston, they drove past stretches of forests and green pastures, where herds of cattle were grazing.

"Some of the cows grazing there are being raised for brisket," informed Richie.

"Not cows, city boy! They're steers."

"What's the difference?"

"Cows are female cattle, raised for milking and producing calves; steers are castrated at an early age and are raised for beef. A rancher or farmer usually keeps only one bull to impregnate a whole herd of cows. The rest eventually end up on someone's table."

"Poor steers," responded Richie. "So, were you raised on a farm, Brio?"

"No, I wasn't raised on a farm, but I spent a lot of time on farms. My father was a farm manager, and my grandmother lived on a farm in Nebraska. She once taught me how to behead a chicken, remove its feathers, butcher it, and prepare it for dinner. Her fried chicken was delicious, but her specialty was *Schwarzsauer*, a

German soup with goose and dried fruit stewed in a broth. She served it with home-baked bread. Yum!"

"My grandmother's specialty was a blackberry dessert, sort of a cross between pudding and dessert, sort of a cross between pudding and Jell-O. It was made with fresh blackberries, water, sugar, and –

"Gelatin?"

"Could be. I remember, it was summertime, and I asked my mother to make it. 'No,' she said, 'it takes too much time. Ask your grandmother to make it.' So, I walked over to my grandmother's house in the afternoon and begged her to make it. 'O.K.' she said. 'Go to the market early tomorrow and get as many blackberries as you can carry. I'll make a big batch so it will last you a while.' She began making it the next morning and stood all day stirring it in a big pot. From time to time, she let me sample it. When it was ready, about four in the afternoon, she dished up a big bowl for me and watched me gulp it down. She gave me the rest in the pot to take home. It was my dessert for about a month."

"A *sweet* story," remarked Brio. "Your grandmother sounds like a *sweet* lady."

"You remind me of her, Brio."

When they reached Houston, Richie drove to the Marriott Marquis Hotel, located on Walker Street in the downtown area. The approach to the modern structure was a very wide driveway, which spanned the length of the building. Inside, the spacious lobby also extended the length of the hotel. A huge crystal chandelier, resembling hanging icicles, enhanced the modern décor. As Richie went to the desk to register, Brio had her choice of dozens of seats.

They took the elevator to their guestroom on the eighth floor, in the taller section of the hotel. (A lower section led to the swimming pool.) As they entered their room, Brio was impressed with its sleek appearance.

"Let's unpack and change into our suits for a swim," suggested Richie.

"Will we be going out for dinner this evening?" asked Brio. "If so, I need to hang up my dress."

"Of course. Tonight, we will celebrate."

When they walked into the pool area after changing, Richie apparently knew his way around. It was a huge area, with cabanas and enough lounging chairs for a multitude of people. A covered bar was located near the door; there was a firepit nearby in an open-air section. There were two pools for swimming, one was a large rectangular pool with a deep-water section for diving and a view of the city; the other was called a "lazy river," which wound around the area, like a serpent in the shape of the state of Texas. It was deep enough for either swimming or wading. Brio began by wading in the "lazy river," and Richie chose the rectangular pool for rapid swimming back and forth. They met near the bar to sunbathe and have a drink.

"Enjoying it here?" Richie asked.

"It's delightful," Brio answered.

"Good. I've made reservations for dinner tonight at the Grotto Downtown Restaurant. Do you like Italian food, Brio?"

"Yes, I love Italian food. Is the restaurant close to the hotel?"

"Within walking distance. There's a park nearby where we can stroll before dinner."

For the evening, Richie dressed in an expensive light brown suit, a white dress shirt, a maroon tie, and brown loafers. Brio wore a peach-colored pantsuit and black pumps. They walked to The Grotto, a short distance from the hotel. The restaurant was crowded but not too noisy for good conversation.

"You chose an Italian restaurant for tonight," said Brio. "Why did you leave Italy to come to the U.S.?"

"I didn't leave to come to the U.S. I left Italy to start a job at the United Nations in Geneva."

"Oh, what was your job?"

"I was an assistant to an official. My job was to go to a country having problems in trade, to learn more about the trouble and how to resolve it. I traveled throughout Europe and the Middle East."

"Sounds interesting."

"It was, but a lot of traveling and living out of a suitcase."

For dinner, they agreed upon chicken piccata, risotto, a salad, and glasses of Sauvignon Blanc.

"We'll have dessert later," promised Richie. As they left the restaurant, the city lights seemed to sparkle, the air was warm and soft, and a splashing fountain added to the music of the evening.

"It's been a lovely evening," Brio remarked.

"It's not over yet," responded Richie, with a squeeze of her hand.

Upon entering the room, Brio saw a round candle-topped cake on the dresser, a bottle of champagne, and two glasses.

"How did you do this?" she asked.

"I have my ways."

He brought out his lighter and lit the candles.

"Happy birthday, Brio. And many more."

"I don't know about more. I am already too old for you, Richie."

"You're still beautiful, Brio. You are a very interesting mature woman. I feel that age isn't everything."

"What **is** then?"

"To me, it's the ability to be a friend, a sister, a mother and sometimes, a lover. The young women I know don't have that ability."

"Maybe you just haven't looked hard enough."

Richie shook his head. Brio lifted her champagne glass and said, "Here's to you, Richie. I hope you find what you're looking for."

"I will. Cheers!"

The next day went by quickly, with breakfast in the hotel, a quick swim, a business appointment for Richie in Houston, and a stop at Buc-ee's for brisket sandwiches on the way home.

"Mickey, I'm home!" Brio called as she entered the condo. Mickey sauntered into the living room and settled down on her lap to watch a movie with her. As Brio crawled into bed that night, she felt that the curse of Covid was beginning to lose its hold on her.

Chapter V

Business Deals

Brio was looking forward to days of happiness in San Antonio. As usual, the weather was sunny and bright, but Brio's life lacked contentment. Richie was very busy, but he managed to fit her into his schedule by inviting himself for brunch, the only part of the day he had free. Brio usually prepared omelets with several kinds of cheese, toast, fresh fruit, and strong coffee. They ate on the deck, with Mickey in attendance.

"I wish I had some music out here," said Brio as they sipped their coffee.

"I've noticed your baby grand in the living room. Do you play?"

"Yes, I started playing at age five and graduated from a music conservatory at fifteen. Music has been an important part of my life."

"I play a little guitar, but I never had lessons. My parents were struggling to survive."

"Survive what? A war?"

"No. My father had a kidney operation, and the anesthetic left him in a coma for six months."

Mickey interrupted the conversation by singing in "*cat-ese*" to a bird perched on an overhanging branch.

"That's a pretty song, Mickey, but I think Brio needs a sound system installed." Mickey ignored Richie's comment, but Brio responded to it.

"Here on the patio?"

"Yes, and throughout the house, a surround system with ceiling speakers and servers. I'll write out a proposal and come by to explain it," he said as Brio escorted him to the front door.

Two weeks later, the installation of the surround sound system began. Because of the mess that would be created, Richie had arranged for Brio to stay at the Marriott Resort in the Hill Country for a vacation paid by his company. Brio pictured the stay as another joyful time.

The resort was located in an area with numerous oaktrees and green meadows. The hotel consisted of six large connected sections and three separate buildings, enclosing a central garden. At the resort, there were four pools, a lazy river, lagoons, fountains, water slides, a spa, lounging areas, walking trails, tennis courts, and a golf course.

Brio's room, situated on an upper floor of the hotel, had a picture window which opened to a balcony, with a beautiful view of a pool and patio area, surrounded by banks of flowering bushes.

"Idyllic!" remarked Brio. "Shall we go for a swim?"

"You can. This is a holiday for you; for me, it's work."

Richie stayed only long enough to give Brio a tour. His knowledge of the hotel and grounds convinced Brio that he had brought customers there in the past.

As the week unfolded, Brio did her best to entertain herself. Not wanting to take advantage of Richie's generosity, she paid for all food and personal expenses herself. The pool was free, and she spent most of her time swimming in the pool, wading in the lazy river, or lounging poolside. Because of Covid, guests were required to wear masks inside and to stay six feet apart. Cibolo, the main restaurant, was open only at limited times, but room service was available in the guest rooms. Usually, Brio ordered from a limited menu in her room. She took the meal out onto the balcony, with Mickey as her companion. (Richie had encouraged Brio to bring Mickey and had set up arrangements for his stay.) All in all, Brio spent a lonely week in beautiful surroundings.

When the installation of the sound system was completed and Brio was back in her condo, Richie invited himself for brunch. Since it was raining, they ate at the kitchen table.

"You seem depressed," commented Brio. "Weather getting you down?"

"No. Divorce."

"You're married?"

"Yes, but Mandie and I have been estranged for a year. We've each been living in different parts of our condo. Now she is insisting that I move out."

"Do you have children?"

"Mandie has two from her first marriage; I am only the stepdad."

"Did you have a prior marriage?"

"No, but I was engaged to an Italian girl in Genoa."

"What happened?"

"She left me for a man with a flashy sports car."

"Nice!"

Richie grimaced. "I saw them together ten years later when I was there on vacation. He was still driving the same car, looking beat up, and she was no longer beautiful."

"Physical beauty doesn't last," responded Brio.

Richie studied Brio before speaking.

"I'd like to stay here a while. What do you think?"

"No. You're not divorced yet. I don't want to get involved. Why don't you get your own place?" Richie frowned but agreed to do that.

Richie moved a bed into his business office for temporary living quarters. Brio invited him to her condo when he needed to shower, and he brought over his shaving gear, toiletries, and several changes of clothes, which Brio laundered for him. He looked for apartments or condos to rent or to buy, but none seemed a good choice. Some were too expensive. Those he could afford lacked one or more of his requirements: good location, adequate living quarters, a spacious garage, and no restrictions about pets. Richie couldn't live without Maya and Basha!

When Richie needed to go to Houston again, he invited Brio along. "Thanks for helping me out this past month," he said as they headed out of San Antonio.

"I remember what it was like when I was living on my own as a young teacher and then later in life after my husband died," Brio remarked. Richie reached out and tousled Brio's hair, bringing a slight smile to her face. A conversation about Brio's marriage to Ben followed.

When they reached Houston, Richie drove to a beautiful residential area where the houses were separated by large lawns. Each was a custom house with artistic architectural features.

"Now, that's what I call a home," commented Richie as he parked. During his call upon the client, Brio sat in the car and read a novel she had brought along. For dinner, they went to Brio's choice: Papadoux, a seafood restaurant featuring southern cuisine. As they headed back to San Antonio, Richie described a house that he was interested in buying: a custom, two-story brick home on one-half acre of land in a gated community; it would be ideal for living and working at home.

"It would be a good investment for *you*, Brio."

"Why me? It would be *your* house."

"You could make interest from a private loan to me."

"Why don't you get a bank loan?"

"A private loan would benefit both you and me. Banks charge high interest rates for the borrowers and pay low rates for loaners. I could give you a much better rate and we could draw up our own terms."

"You're right. Banks give a measly rate of interest on all savings."

When they arrived at Brio's condo, Richie walked her to the door, kissed her, and said, "I'll call you in a few days. Think about the investment."

When Richie called, Brio had not made up her mind. She asked him to set up a time with the realtor when she could see the property. Richie explained that renters would be there until the end of the month, but he would contact the realtor and establish a visiting time.

Richie called for Brio on Saturday morning and drove northwest for thirty minutes to reach the area. He had an opener for the gate into the development. The house, located at the bottom of a cul-de-sac, was a white brick home with a large two-car garage on a pie-shaped lot; in the back were a lawn, pool, patio, and cabana.

"We only have fifteen minutes before the renters come back," warned Richie as he opened the front door. A two-story spacious entrance with a curved stairway greeted them. To the right of the entrance was a living room, to the left a study, to the back a very large kitchen/family room with a fireplace. A half-bath was adjacent to the family room, and a laundry room next to the kitchen. Upstairs was the master bedroom suite, with a walk-in closet and a bathroom with double sinks, granite countertops, a tub, and a shower big enough for two. Two smaller bedrooms, separated by a bathroom, and a double-size bedroom completed the second floor.

"Well, it's certainly designed well," remarked Brio as they entered the car. "I noticed, though, that it hasn't been well cared for. The carpet is dirty and spotted, the walls and woodwork need painting, and the hardwood in the upstairs hall and on the stairs needs refinishing."

"Yes," agreed Richie. "I could do most of that myself."

Several days later, Richie brought Brio a contract and an amortized schedule of payments.

"I can take you to the bank for a cashier's check made out to me and then to the notary to sign the papers," said Richie.

"I hope this will be a good investment," responded Brio, but she was thinking that a lot of her money was getting tied up with Richie; first the computer, then the sound system, and now a house.

During October, November, and December, Brio saw little of Richie. He was busy at work, and in his spare time, he was working on the house. He painted the inside, put up shelving in the garage, refinished the hardwood, added lighting and cameras on the patio, and installed a security system inside the house.

"Can we spend time together at Christmas?" Brio asked.

"In the security business, the holiday time is a busy time. That's when customers want to have work done. Besides, I need to spend time with Mandie's son and daughter; I'm still their stepdad. But cheer up, Brio! After Christmas, I'll have time!"

Brio was disappointed. She could see another lonely Christmas ahead.

Chapter VI

How Could He?

On a sunny day in January, Richie came for Brio in his vintage Mercedes for an outing. Their destination was Fredericksburg, a small town seventy miles away. Taking Highway 10 Northwest, Richie drove through the Leon Valley. At Helotes, he pointed in the direction of a hill and said, "I own land there, which is inaccessible by car, but it should be more valuable when this area is developed."

The next town they drove through was Boerne, where Richie pointed out the old structures dating back to the mid-1800s.

"We're headed for Fredericksburg," Richie said. "It has buildings like these but better preserved. This whole area was founded by German immigrants who left Prussia when it was ruled by Prince Frederick."

"Oh, all of my ancestors emigrated from Prussia, some as early as 1860," Brio informed him.

"We're going there *because* of your German ancestors, Brio." She nodded and asked him why the area had not been Americanized. Richie explained that the first generations of settlers had refused to speak English, and the following generations carried on their traditions and refused to blend in with Americans. Consequently, Fredericksburg is still called "the German town of Texas." Entering the town, Richie drove past the Pioneer Memorial Library, located in Courthouse Square. A flower-bordered pathway led to the entrance of a two-story, chiseled-stone building that had been the former courthouse before the building was converted into the library.

"It's beautiful," remarked Brio. "I like the combination of Roman and Gothic-style windows, typical of European architecture a century ago." Next, Richie drove past a family home built in 1870, in the style of the Old West, a two-story wooden house with upper and lower porches. In the vicinity were an old pharmacy built in 1906 and the White Elephant Saloon constructed in 1888.

"Want to shop in a few boutique stores on Main Street?" asked Richie. Brio nodded. On the way, they passed by a park with a bandstand. Richie explained that German music was still played there and musicians in folk costumes danced and sang.

"Hungry yet?" Richie asked.

"Yes, I'm ready for *Wienerschnitzel* (a breaded veal cutlet), red fermented cabbage, and potato pancakes." Richie drove to the Altdorf Restaurant and Biergarten, which was bound to have these dishes on the menu.

When they finished eating, Brio playfully said, "*Danke schoen. Alles schmeckt.*"

"Say again?" said Richie.

"Thank you very much. Everything tasted good," she repeated in translation.

On the seventy-mile return trip to San Antonio, Richie relayed his plans for a new business venture. He would like to start a second company that would become a subsidiary of My Computer Technology, with the same owners, managers, and employees. The new company would buy a house to "flip." After renovating it, they would sell it and reinvest the profit in another house to flip.

"The property I want to purchase is on King Road. It's not a good area, but it's a Spanish community, where people know each other. I have the money for the cost of the renovation, but I need *seed money* to purchase the house," explained Richie. "Think about it, Brio; it's a good money-maker."

Brio took several days to get back to Richie. She thought about the programs she had watched on T.V., describing "flipping houses." The project would require good laborers and a knowledgeable boss. Richie was definitely that. He was skilled in all types of construction and capable of instructing laborers who needed guidance. He was also dependable. He had never missed a payment to her on his house loan.

Richie invited Brio for lunch at La Madeleine, a bakery and café near her condo. Over quiche and salad, they discussed the new venture. It would be called B and R Home Services, standing for Brio and Richie. Richie would apply to Secretary of State in Texas for LLC status so that Brio's condo would be protected against a lawsuit or financial disaster. Brio promised to have money available for the purchase of "King" on January 7th. B and R Services was being launched!

All went well during January. The technical employees at My Computer Technology were willing and able to handle the workload in the computer division as well as the manual labor needed at B and R Home Services. However, when Covid became less of a threat and technical business increased, Richie had to hire manual laborers to work on the King renovation. Good manual workers were difficult to find. Some preferred to stay at home and subsist on government hand-outs; some were unskilled and made expensive mistakes; some were lazy and accomplished little; some showed up late or left early; some didn't show up at all. More than one employee stole expensive equipment, putting the job on hold until new equipment arrived. Richie charged the equipment to his credit card account, but by mid-March, he had run out of cash to make payroll. Since Brio was part owner of the firm, he turned to her for help. She paid for payroll twice, but the third time, she balked.

Richie was going to Houston for business on April 16th. He asked Brio to accompany him so that they could discuss work problems. At the last minute, without explanation, he cancelled and drove to Houston alone. Brio was angry and upset. She was worried about the loss of money for Richie and for herself, and she was concerned about Richie's treatment of her. Two days later, Richie visited her unexpectedly at the condo. He offered no explanation for cancelling the trip, and he was in a belligerent mood and on the verge of losing control. Brio misjudged him and pressed him for answers which he did not (or could not) give.

"I need you to shut up!" he finally yelled and began heading for the door.

"I need you to answer and explain!" she yelled in return.

"O.K. Come with me!" he ordered. He led the way upstairs and into the walk-in closet of the master bedroom, where the upstairs server to the sound system was located.

"What's wrong with the server?" Brio asked.

"Shut up! I told you to shut up!"

"I was just… "

She was unable to finish her sentence. Richie had taken ahold of her ear with one hand and slapped her face with the other.

"Don't!" She recoiled.

"Are you going to shut up?"

Brio stood transfixed, afraid to utter a sound.

"Next time, I'll kill you," threatened Richie. He bounded down the stairs and out of the condo.

Brio was shaken. She stood quietly for a while, trying to still her pounding heart. Then she examined her face in the mirror and found the red marks from the slaps. She doused her face with cold water and then went downstairs to curl up on the couch. Mickey, who had no doubt heard the shouting, came in to console her. He jumped up and licked her hands.

"How *could* he do that to me," she whimpered. But it was only her own thoughts that answered her. She had in no way been responsible for his employee or money problems; she had given him money to meet the payroll and the "seed money" to start the company. It made no sense to her. It was like "biting the hand that feeds you." She wondered if the stress of his business problems had been too much for him to handle, causing him to snap, like a rubber band stretched too far.

As Mickey cuddled in bed with her, she hugged him. "You're a sweet, sweet boy, Mickey," she said softly, realizing that they would tomorrow be alone again.

Chapter VII

Separation

During the following months of separation from Richie, Brio analyzed her personal and financial situation. She realized that she should not remain at Alamo Heights. Living alone was dangerous; she should be in a gated community. She contacted a realtor to put her condo on the market and to find her a residence where she would be safe. Silvie showed her many places for sale or for rent but, like Richie, Brio could not find one that she liked. In the condo in Alamo Heights, she had been able to arrange her antique furniture, Persian rugs, and collectibles in a decorative way that was pleasing to her. The baby grand piano required a large living room, hard to find in a condo. Furthermore, she would miss the shops and small neighborhood atmosphere of Alamo Heights.

Silvie finally suggested a "new build," a house instead of a condo, in a gated community. She drove Brio to see the models at Freedom Homes, located forty miles from the center of San Antonio. The model that interested Brio was a one-story stucco and brick structure, with a two-car garage. It had a spacious entrance hall, a large living/family room (perfect for the baby grand), a kitchen, a den with French doors, a master bedroom suite with a walk-in closet and a master bathroom, a second bathroom and bedroom for guests, and a laundry room. Brio would be able to select the tile for the floors, the granite for the countertops in the kitchen and bathrooms, and the brick for the fireplace. The lot would be landscaped with a patio in the backyard, a large lawn with sprinklers, and several trees and bushes.

The house would be ready by the end of December. It would cost half as much as the Alamo Heights condo and the property taxes would be $7,000 a year instead of $13,000. Furthermore, there would be no HOA fees of $700 per month.

"This is nicer than my condo and much less expensive," remarked Brio to Silvie.

"The cost is lower because of the location," explained Silvie. "Alamo Heights is an established neighborhood with mature landscaping and older, stately homes, and it is closer to the center of town. This is a new community, forty miles away, farther to commute to businesses and offices."

"Ah, location, location, location," quipped Brio.

When Richie discovered that Brio had made a down payment on a "new build," he called and reminded her that they were still business partners. She owed him the opportunity of finding her a place that would be closer and even financially better for her. Besides, he was still paying her for the private loan on his house. Since Brio was concerned that he might stop making his loan payments, she allowed him to show her places for sale. Although the search continued throughout the summer and into the fall, Brio did not see anything better than the model house at Freedom Homes, and Richie became increasingly annoyed.

Finally, Richie tried a different approach to win back Brio. He invited her to help him celebrate his birthday. He chose a romantic setting for the occasion: a dinner at the Tower of the Americas, a 750-foot tower on Chavez Boulevard in Hemisfair Park in San Antonio. A wide, brick walkway led to the tower. Bordered by flowers and trees, it went under an arched metal bridge and past a fountain, with water cascading down steps. Richie stopped by the fountain and asked Brio to pose with him for a picture with his cell camera. She was wearing black silk pants and a loose, bright blouse with the colors of red, gold, and black. He was attired in black trousers and a fashionable white dress shirt.

"A good-looking couple," he remarked, showing her the photo.

They strolled around the park before heading to the needle for the 750-foot elevator ride to the top. The dome at the top was circular, with a bar in the center and tables and chairs next to tall picture windows, overlooking the city below. The table reserved for them was not adjacent to the windows, but it was close enough to see the skyscrapers and lower buildings of San Antonio. At first, it was early enough to see the vista clearly; later, a brilliant sunset flashed across the sky, followed by the city lights.

Throughout dinner, Richie avoided the topic of business. As they sipped their liqueurs and coffee, Richie revealed that he was scheduled for extensive oral surgery for implants in the entire section of his upper jaw. First, there would be preliminary visits and exams. Then his teeth would be extracted and temporary teeth implanted on the same day. He would need at least three days of help during the recovery period. A return visit to the oral surgeon would follow, to determine how healing was progressing. When the gums and bones were healed enough, the surgeon would implant the permanent teeth. The entire process would take four to six months. In the meantime, Richie's diet would be limited to liquids and soft foods.

"Wow!" said Brio.

"I'm afraid," admitted Richie. "I'm not sure I can handle the recovery period alone."

"Don't you have someone to be with you?"

"Only you." Brio shook her head. "You know, Brio, there have been several times in my life when I've had to face danger and fear alone."

"When was that?"

"When I was in primary school in Syria. My mother's family were living in Lebanon, but we were in Syria, where my father was forced to work as a civil engineer, building roads. My three brothers and I were bullied by our Syrian classmates, who hated the Lebanese. By cow-towing to the bullies, my brothers stayed out of trouble, but I wouldn't cow-tow. My parents thought that I was a troublemaker because I chose to defend myself. So, I was on my own."

"Did you get beaten up?"

"Yes. Three or four guys cornered me after school. My brothers ran away, and I was beaten almost to death. After that, I started carrying a long iron bar."

"For defense?"

"Yes. When they managed to corner me, I struck back with the bar; I got to be an expert at handling it. I produced a lot of bruises, gashes, and even a broken head once. They eventually left me alone."

"I'm sorry you went through that, Richie. But I'm glad you survived."

"Thanks. I'll be pretty defenseless when I'm recovering from the surgery. I'll be on strong pain pills, perhaps unconscious at times, incapable of caring for myself. Will you help me out, Brio? I trust you."

"Yes, I'll help you through it."

Four days later, Richie and a chauffeur called for Brio with a limousine that had a bed and a long bench in the back. When they got to Houston, the chauffeur waited during the four-hour period of examination, x-rays, surgery, and recovery. Afterward, he helped Richie from the surgeon's office back into the limousine. During the 200-mile ride home, Richie lay on the bed, almost unconscious from pain and medication. Brio sat beside him and nursed him as he alternated between fever and chills. When they reached Brio's condo, the chauffeur helped Richie up the stairs and into the guest bedroom.

Brio took care of Richie for the next sixty hours. For the first twelve hours, he was helpless. Brio did all she could for him. She removed the cotton wads from his mouth, put in fresh wads, gave him an antiseptic solution for rinsing, and emptied the metal bowl he used for spitting. She brought him fresh water to drink and his pain medication, which she kept track of. When he called her, she helped him to the bathroom to urinate and then back into bed.

The next day his condition was only a little improved. She checked on him every two hours and did what was needed, but she did not disturb him. Towards the evening, he was ready for cool liquids. On the fourth day, Richie was able to go home to complete his recovery alone. As Brio drove him home, he expressed his gratitude.

"No one has ever been so kind to me, Brio. You've been an angel." Brio smiled and nodded.

"Brio, I once described the perfect woman: she has the ability to be a friend, a sister, a mother, and a lover." He tousled her hair. "And an angel." Brio pulled into Richie's driveway.

"Take care of yourself, Richie; rest and recover."

"I will. And Brio, I wish you'd cancel the *new build* and let me find a solution to our finances. I'm so sorry about everything, and I'm convinced now that you really do care about me."

Chapter VIII

Relationship Rekindled?

On November 9th, Brio took her condo off the market and cancelled her contract with Freedom Homes. A week later, Brio and Richie had dinner together at the condo. Since it was chilly outside, they ate at the kitchen table. Richie repeated his expression of thanks for Brio's nursing.

"No one has ever been so kind to me, Brio. You've been my friend, my sister, and my mother all rolled into one." He paused. "Can we add *lover* to that list?"

"We'll see," answered Brio.

The evening progressed with a bottle of wine, Brio's choice of easy listening music, and conversation about Paris. Brio commented that she had visited Paris as a young woman, had fallen in love with the city, and had always wanted to return.

"I know Paris well," said Richie. "It was close enough to go there during a weekend when we lived in Genoa. Later, when I worked at the UN in Geneva, it was close enough for a day."

"So, you know your way around in the city?"

"Yes, the streets of the left and right bank, the entertainment spots, and the restaurants. It truly is a city for creating memories."

"I have good memories of Paris, too, and a few mementos: two watercolors, an antique French pendulum clock, and a glass bottle of Chanel No.5. (The perfume by now is *long gone*.)"

"You don't need the perfume, Brio."

Later that evening, as Richie was leaving to go home, he remarked, "Tonight, we added *lover* to the list of nouns for the perfect woman; and, I hope, for the perfect man."

"I'm far from perfect, Richie."

"I guess I am, too. So, good night." As he gave Brio a goodnight hug, she winced.

"Are you O.K.?"

"Yes, it's nothing. Good night."

Three days later, Brio went to Dr. Stellmann because of pains in her left wrist, forearm, and right chest area. The doctor ordered x-rays, which showed a sprained wrist and forearm and hairline fractures to two upper ribs. "The rib fractures explain your chest pain," he said. "They will knit together on their own. Just avoid lifting and upper body exercise."

When Brio explained her injuries to Richie, he said quietly, "Sorry." Changing the subject, he said, "I have a trip planned for Paris next week. Is your passport up-to-date?" Brio assured him that it was and that she would start getting ready to travel. She found a cat sitter for Mickey, made a list of clothing and toiletries to pack, and inquired about shots and health papers needed for airline passengers. Brio determined which pieces of luggage to take, but she left them unpacked until she heard from Richie regarding the itinerary and departure date.

However, when Richie called, it was to inform her of a change of plans. He was going alone to Europe to bring back to San Antonio his fifteen-year-old niece, Jena, to live with him. He neither offered an explanation nor gave an apology. Brio was shocked and hurt.

"Au Revoir!" she shouted angrily.

Two weeks later, Richie invited Brio for a steak dinner at his house on Thanksgiving Day. Brio declined. Richie called again and pleaded with her. "Jena really wants to meet you. I've told her so much about you." Richie explained that the decision to bring Jena to San Antonio had been a family one, not just his. Jena had had a tough life and needed kindness shown to her.

"Give her a chance, Brio."

"I'll come for one dinner," promised Brio.

When she arrived at Richie's house in the early evening, he introduced Jena and Brio and then led them out to the patio where a fire was burning in the brick grill. It was a romantic setting, with pool lights on, candles on the wicker tables, and a bottle of red wine waiting to be poured. Richie attended to the grilling of the steaks, the garlic bread, and the tossed salad as Brio and Jena got acquainted. Brio learned that Jena had been living with her grandparents. Her father and mother were divorced. Jena's father (Richie's brother) had remarried and now had two younger children with his second wife who did not want Jena living with them. Nor did Jena's mother. So, she had been taken in by her grandparents (Richie's father and mother). His parents had encouraged Richie to take on the role of stepdad to Jena.

As they sat on the wicker couch, Jena said, "My dad (Richie) really likes you. Do you like him?"
"I don't know. I used to, "Brio answered.

"He's always been good to me. Whenever he came to visit us, he always spent time with me."

"Well, I need someone closer to my age, someone who has time for me."

"Age isn't everything," Jena said, glancing quickly at Richie. *Where have I heard that before*, thought Brio. *She's young, but is she a manipulator?* Richie had been facing the grill and had his back to the wicker couch, but Brio could tell that he had been listening to their conversation. He remained quiet throughout the dinner, letting fifteen-year-old Jena act as hostess.

Throughout December, Richie pursued Brio as his "friend" and his "sister." However, whenever Paris was mentioned, he sounded more like a "lover." On December 16th, he brought Brio a bottle of perfume, called "I Love Paris," and proposed a Christmas vacation trip to Paris for just the two of them (He would make arrangements for Jena's care at home.)

"I especially want you to visit the Eiffel Tower with me, Brio. Paris can work wonders for relationships."

Brio wondered if the plan to fly to Paris would transpire for her this time. However, when she heard from Richie that he had purchased the airline tickets, she felt assured. He sent her the itinerary:

United Airlines – San Antonio to Atlanta, December 24, 2021

Delta Airlines – Atlanta to Paris, overnight flight, arriving December 25

Five days in Paris, December 25 – 29

Delta Airlines – Paris to Atlanta, overnight flight, arriving December 30

United Airline – Atlanta to San Antonio, December 30

With two days of travel, we will have only five days in Paris, not much time for sightseeing, thought Brio. *I'll have to make a list of what I want to see in such a short time.*

During the next week, Brio remembered that she had several books about Paris and its environs, including a huge volume she had purchased when she was married to Ben. (She had always wanted Ben to take her there. She romantically believed that Paris was most enjoyed by lovers. But Ben, who considered himself a photographer, always wanted to go to a spot that he hadn't already seen.) As Brio studied the book about Paris and another about the charming villages and countryside surrounding Paris, she took a few notes, thinking that Richie and she might take a day's excursion outside of Paris.

The night before they left for Paris, Brio packed. Since the trip was so short, she packed only a small suitcase with clothes and a carry-on bag for toiletries. As she closed the lid to the suitcase, she thought about Richie's statement: *Paris can work wonders for relationships.*

Chapter IX

Paris

On December 24th, Richie came for Brio in the Lincoln SUV and drove to the San Antonio Airport, where they boarded a United plane for Atlanta. There they transferred to Delta for the overnight trip to Paris. As they entered the first-class cabin, they saw three sections of seats.

Richie was seated in the left section. A middle section separated him from Brio's seat in the right section. Brio immediately asked the stewardess to change her seat so that she could be near Richie. "Don't make a fuss, Brio," Richie chastised her. "It doesn't matter." She responded, "I think it does." When Brio persisted, the stewardess quickly found another passenger willing to change seats. Richie and Brio were now seated across a narrow aisle from each other.

For each passenger, there was a separate cubicle that contained a small desk, a tray table, media devices, a storage area, and a spacious seating area, which enabled a range of upright positions for sitting and a stretched-out position for sleeping. Each seating area had been constructed to give passengers either privacy or communication and to enable them to feel protected from Covid.

As soon as the plane reached its cruising altitude, the steward served champagne and hors d'oeuvres. Richie turned on his T.V. and ignored Brio. After the movie, he took a nap. When dinner started, he was fast asleep. Brio asked the stewardess to wake him so that he wouldn't miss the meal. Following dinner, passengers settled down to read, listen to music, watch T.V., or to sleep. Richie settled down without bidding Brio goodnight.

Shortly after breakfast had been served, the plane landed. Richie and Brio collected their luggage from the baggage area and picked up the SUV that Richie had reserved. It was Christmas Day and traffic on the highway and streets of Paris was heavy. Their hotel was located on a narrow cobblestone street, located not far from the Parc du Champs de Mars, which was a long swath of grassy area that extended southeast for several blocks towards the Eiffel Tower. Richie had chosen the hotel for its affordability and its proximity to the tower. They checked in at the hotel, left their bags in the lobby, and drove to an underground garage located a block away. Because of the pedestrian traffic on the narrow sidewalk, they walked in the middle of the cobblestone street as they returned to the hotel. Brio looked for a glimpse of the Eiffel Tower, but there was none.

As they entered their room on the fourth floor, Richie exclaimed, "It's really small!" It had a double bed, a night stand, a desk with a chair, and a small area with an open bar for hanging clothes and a few shelves. To look out the six-foot by four-foot window, they would have to step past their suitcases, which would remain on the floor. The small bathroom contained a very small shower with a hand-held faucet, a toilet (W.C.), and a pedestal sink with no mirror above. *Cramped and not designed for romance*, thought Brio.

"Let's unpack and then go downstairs for a drink," suggested Richie. "I noticed a bar in the lobby."

The lobby was only large enough for a reception desk, the bar, and a few chairs in the corner of the room. Off the lobby were a breakfast room with two long tables and an open-air patio, which no one was using in December. Since Richie needed a place to smoke, he and Brio sat on the cold patio while they had their drinks.

In the early evening, as they headed toward the Eiffel Tower on the Champ de Mars, Brio asked, "Did you know that the engineer of the Eiffel Tower was not a Frenchman?"

"No. It's very much French now."

"The engineer was Gustave Eiffel, a German. His company built the tower in 1887 – 1889 for the world's fair. At first, the Parisiennes didn't like it; they thought it looked like an ugly piece of machinery. They only began to like it after it became a landmark of Paris."

"You've been studying about Paris," remarked Richie.

"Yes, in preparation for the trip."

By the time they had parked and walked to the tower area to get their tickets, the evening was no longer young. They waited in line for the elevator, which would take them to a platform halfway up the tower. (The platform near the top was closed for renovation.)

"Just my luck," said Brio. "When I was in Milan several years ago, the outside of the cathedral was covered with scaffolding. Some of the huge stained-glass windows were —-"

Ignoring Brio, Richie turned from her to ask a pretty young woman standing behind them if she was French. She nodded but answered in English. He inquired about the renovation and she explained that the renovation was scheduled to continue for some time.

"Have you ever been to the U.S.?" asked Richie. She responded that she hadn't but perhaps would someday do that. Richie reached into the pocket of his jacket and handed her his business card.

"Well, if you do," he said, "look me up. I'll be glad to show you around." The woman looked quickly at Brio to see her reaction and then took his card. (Brio had not reacted.)

Later, when Brio and Richie stood at the railing of the platform, Richie pointed out to her what he thought were the lights of the Arc de Triomphe, off in the distance, and the nearer lights of the skyscrapers of La Defense, the Parisienne business district.

"I'll be taking pictures," he said and walked away with his cell phone in his hand. Brio stopped at each telescopic location around the circular platform. She did not know what she was viewing, but the lights of Paris were spectacular. Close to the time when the elevator would be closing, Richie returned. He guided her to a somewhat secluded spot and put on her finger a ring in the shape of the Eiffel Tower. It had a large two-carat marquis-shaped diamond, a smaller round diamond, and tiny diamonds on the sides leading to the peak of the ring.

"You brought this with you?" she asked.

"Yes, I wanted to give it to you here."

"But you were just flirting with that pretty, young woman." Richie smiled.

"Sorry, that was naughty of me."

To celebrate their engagement, Richie drove until he found a restaurant which appeared to have a pleasant Parisienne ambience. It was an excellent choice. After an evening of fresh, crisp air at the Eiffel Tower, the cuisine and wine tasted *superb*. Returning to the hotel, Richie parked the car in the garage, and they crept two floors up in the dim lighting to street level. Brio took hold of Richie's arm to help her on the uneven cobblestones as they walked up the middle of the street to the hotel. Suffering from jet lag, they crawled into bed with a quick kiss and a goodnight.

The next morning, Richie did not want to get up, so Brio went down to the breakfast room alone. Returning to the room, she awakened Richie to make plans for the day. His plan was to sleep. Her plan was to go to the Musee d'Orsay, an art museum which was much smaller than the Louvre, but it had one of the best impressionistic collections of paintings in Paris. Although Brio encouraged Richie to come with her, he preferred to spend the day in bed. However, he promised to drive her there and then return for her later.

Brio did not mind being alone in the art gallery. In fact, she preferred it. She was free to stand or sit in front of a painting for as long as she liked or to ignore it completely or to give it a quick look. The museum contained small collections of Seurat, Pizarro, Sisley, Rousseau, and Matisse, which Brio enjoyed, and larger collections of Monet and Renoir, her favorites. She soaked up the beauty of Monet's landscape scenes of "Poppies" and "Water Lilies," two of his most famous works. Since she had always enjoyed literature from the nineteenth century, the paintings by Renoir, depicting Parisienne life at that time, were like descriptions of scenes from a Victorian novel. She stood for a long time studying "Dance at Le Moulin de la Galette" and "Luncheon of the Boating Party."

After four hours of standing, Brio was ready to get off her feet. Richie, as promised, was waiting in the lobby to take her again to the Eiffel Tower to view Paris by daylight. This time, they were able to recognize various landmarks: the Basilica of the *Sacre Coeur*, the Opera

House, the Pantheon, and the *Rive Seine*, which wandered snakelike throughout Paris, dividing the city between the Left Bank and the Right Bank.

For dinner, Richie drove along the Champs Elysees and stopped and parked, but they couldn't find a suitable Parisienne restaurant. One needed reservations; others had too long a wait time, or were too expensive, or demanded more formal attire than they were wearing. Finally, they gave up on dinner, and strolled along the street until they came to a walk-in *creperie* which, luckily, was a good choice. It was a typical Parisienne experience. Brio ordered a chicken and vegetable crepe and Richie a beef and vegetable crepe. They sat at a table next to the area where the batter was poured onto a very large stone that was heated from underneath. The meat and vegetables were placed on top of the crepes to cook. Then the crepes were folded, browned, and flipped before being removed to a plate. Although the meal had been filling, Richie and Brio wanted to see the waiter's skillful flipping again, so they each ordered a dessert crepe with chocolate and cognac sauce.

Well-stuffed, they headed back to the hotel. Brio, who was suffering from jet lag and a day of standing and walking, went to bed early. Richie, who had slept most of the day, escorted her to the room and left to enjoy the nightlife of Paris.

Chapter X

In the SUV

The next morning, Richie slept late again. Brio got up, breakfasted alone, and took a stroll through the neighborhood. At one point, she was turned around in direction and had trouble finding the short street on which the hotel was located. Walking several blocks out of her way, she was relieved when she finally found her way back. Determined not to let Richie sleep all day, she woke him and encouraged him to take her on a driving tour of Paris in the SUV. He grabbed a croissant and coffee in the bakery adjacent to the hotel and smoked a few cigarettes at a table outside before they started on the jaunt.

Richie had said that he knew Paris well, but he didn't really know much about the famous landmarks. Brio brought the guidebook she had purchased on her stroll and suggested visiting some of the places she had marked. Richie used the GPS to find his way through Paris. As he drove, Brio read about the spots they were driving by.

"The Luxembourg Garden and Palace, with its Baroque architecture, was once the residence of Queen Marie de' Medici. Now it is a legislative building.

"The Pantheon, built between 1764 and 1790 for King Louis XV, was originally intended as a church, but it is now a mausoleum.

"The Conciergerie was formerly a courthouse and prison during the French Revolution, where Queen Marie Antoinette was tried and imprisoned before she was beheaded. Now it is a museum.

"The Notre Dame de Paris Cathedral was constructed in the Gothic style, with rib-vaulted ceilings and stained-glass windows, including its magnificent rose window. Flying buttresses support the massive stone structure. The organ inside the cathedral is one of the largest in Europe, with 8,000 pipes.

"The Arc de Triomphe (the Arc of the Stars) is so named because twelve avenues meet at the arc, like rays of a star. It is a patriotic symbol for the French nation and the site of national parades.

"The Basilica of the Sacre Coeur, a Roman Catholic church, was built on the summit of Montmartre, the highest hill in Paris. This area is the most famous shopping center in Paris."

Richie, who had seemed bored, perked up. Shopping?" Did you say shopping?'

"Yes, so you're awake now," retorted Brio.

"Let's go shopping!" Richie parked and Brio followed him into a clothing store.

"I want to get something for Jena and me," he informed her.

Brio followed him around as he selected items of clothing.

"Let me pay for the things for you, as a thank-you gift," offered Brio. Richie accepted, and they left the store, carrying several big bags of clothing.

It was already getting late, and they had not eaten since breakfast. To avoid driving around again, Brio suggested that they eat at a small café that she had seen near their hotel on her morning stroll. Richie was happy to leave the car in the garage when they returned to the hotel. The food was simple but good, and the house wine seemed perfect with it. The other customers appeared to be locals, who were friendly with the waiters. Walking down the middle of the street back to the hotel, Richie took Brio's hand to steady her on the uneven cobblestones. He escorted her to their room, laid his packages on his suitcase, and said, "I'm going downstairs for a drink." He left without asking Brio to join him.

Brio got ready for bed and settled down to read several chapters of the German novel, Perfume, which she had purchased on her walk. At midnight, she began to feel concerned that Richie had not returned. She dressed and took the elevator down to the lobby. He was neither in the breakfast room nor on the outdoor patio. She described Richie to the bartender and asked if he had seen him. He replied, "Oh, I remember that the gentleman came down in his coat and immediately left the hotel." Brio went back to the room, undressed, put on her pajamas, read another chapter, and turned out the light. When Richie stumbled into the room at 2:00 a.m., Brio was asleep. In his clumsy, drunken state, he awakened her.

"Where have you been?" she asked.

"Out for a ride, to see Paris by night." *That's not all*, thought Brio.

Brio and Richie both slept late the following morning. Brio awoke first, dressed, and went to the bakery for croissants and coffee, which she brought back to the room. Bleary-eyed Richie would have preferred to sleep all day, but Brio had other plans. She had her guidebook in hand and opened it to Provins.

"Let's leave Paris today and take an excursion to Provins," she suggested.

"Where's Provins? What's there to see there?" She read the description from the guidebook:

"Provins is one of the best-preserved medieval towns in France; many of the buildings date back to the twelfth and thirteenth centuries. A castle 'keep' and high stone walls still partly remain around the older part of the city, which was built on a hilltop." Brio explained that Provins was about ninety kilometers from Paris, located in an

agricultural area. "If we get off the main highways onto country roads, we should pass through charming villages," added Brio. Richie agreed that it would be a good change from the busy streets of Paris.

Richie concentrated on the traffic until they had left Paris well behind. When he turned off the highway and onto a country road in the direction of Provins, Brio broke the silence.

"Now that we can chat without the distractions of Paris, let's visit, like we used to on our drives to Houston." Richie nodded.

"Richie, you've shared only bits and pieces of your life. How about a chronology, relaying how the pieces fit together?"

"You really want to hear details about me? A lot of them are unpleasant," he warned.

"No matter," she said.

Richie relayed that he had been born in Al Riyadh, Saudi Arabia, where his father had been working as a civil engineer. At the time, his father was lying comatose in a hospital. He had had a kidney operation, which left him with brain damage that was caused by incorrect administration of anesthesia. Richie's mother had difficulty caring for Richie and his two-year-old brother. Her family was from Lebanon and she knew nobody in Saudi Arabia. Fortunately, a friend of his father helped them to survive until he regained consciousness.

When his father recovered, they moved to be near family in Lebanon where a bloody civil war had started. Innocent people were being massacred. Richie was too young to remember, but his mother later told him about walking on top of dead bodies to get a bucket of water from a fountain. When there was a pause in the fighting, they tried to flee to Genoa, Italy, where his father's family lived. On the way, they were captured by the Syrians, who were enemies of the Lebanese, and taken to Syria. For eight years, they were not allowed to leave. The Syrians needed his father's engineering skills in building roads and bridges, which were constantly being destroyed.

"How old were you when you lived in Syria?" Brio asked.

"Ages four through twelve. The Syrians hated the Lebanese, and my older brother and I, along with my two younger brothers, were bullied by Syrian gangs when we walked to and from school. When I was old enough to fight, I used a long iron bar to fend off my aggressors when they had me cornered."

"You mentioned that to me when you talked about your past. Didn't you get into trouble with the police?"

"Yes, all the time. I had to stay safe from the gangs as well as stay clear of the police. Once, my uncle had to come to my rescue. He helped me to escape across the border back into Lebanon and later helped me to return when the coast was clear."

"So, that was your life all through your elementary years."

"Yes, and into secondary school. When my father went to work in Dubai, I became the protector of the family. I spent more and more time as a street fighter. My older brother would not stand up for himself, and my younger brothers looked to me for protection. When we were finally allowed to leave Syria, we went to Genoa, Italy. Since we were not persecuted there, I settled down into a normal life and attempted to become a better person."

"Did you do well in school then?"

"I had missed a lot of schooling, but I caught up and began to receive high marks. It wasn't all peaches and cream, though."

"What happened?"

"At age eighteen, all boys had to spend a year in military school to prepare for warfare. We were sent to a camp that was run like a prison, with a high barbed-wire fence surrounding the grounds. We were taught to shoot, fight, march, and build survival skills. I couldn't stand the confinement." He pointed to the long scar at the edge of his left eye, which extended up his forehead and down the side of his face. "That's when I got this. Not pretty, is it?"

"Actually, it gives your face originality," answered Brio. "You tried to escape?"

"Yes. At night, by climbing over the barbed-wire fence. I climbed up to the top, but on my way over, I slipped and my face was ripped open. The gash was long and deep and it barely missed my eye. I fell to the ground, blinded from the blood. I tried to stop the bleeding, but I lost consciousness and nearly lost my life. Fortunately, a guard saw me and came to my rescue."

"You *did* survive," said Brio.

"Yes, but it took me several months to recover. The military school could have forced me back into their program, but they probably decided that I lacked discipline to follow orders. They sent me home to finish my schooling."

"What a story!" exclaimed Brio. "Your parents were no doubt relieved when you graduated from secondary school."

"Particularly my father. He wanted me to study civil engineering in college, to follow in his footsteps, like two of my brothers, but I was interested in computer science. Instead, I got industrial degrees from a number of companies: Comptia, Cisco, Microsoft. Later, I got a bachelor's degree in Information Systems and then a master's in Information Technology."

"So, you changed from a street fighter to a respectable citizen," said Brio. Richie nodded.

As they approached Provins, Richie said, "I'm tired of talking. I'll tell you the rest of the story some other time." Richie parked the car in a visitors' lot. As they walked into Ville-Basse, the lower town of Provins, Brio began relaying information from her guide book: "*Provins was founded in the ninth century by monks fleeing from the Normans. During the Middle Ages, the town was an economic center and the cite of fairs, where furs and agricultural products were sold. Many old shops and restaurants still exist in the lower town, along with houses of exposed timbers and stucco (similar to those from the Elizabethan period in England). Some structures and roads are made of stone; along with colorful hanging baskets of flowers, they add to the charm of the town.*"

"I see," said Richie, sounding somewhat bored.

In the upper town, the Ville-Haute, Brio led Richie into a large, old stone church, which looked like a Gothic cathedral. Since Richie had never entered a Christian church or cathedral, she escorted him around the interior, pointing out the different parts of the building: the massive stone pillars supporting the vaulted ceiling, the stained-glass windows, the nave and chancel, and the side chapels. Then she explained different aspects of the church that related to the worshippers: the altar and crucifix, the communion railing and kneelers, the pulpit and lectern, and the rows of wooden chairs.

"What's this?" asked Richie, opening the door to a confessional, located in a side aisle. Brio explained the act of a parishioner's confession and the priest's act of conferring absolution for sins.

"I don't believe that a priest can forgive someone for wrongdoing," commented Richie. "I think that a person can do that by himself by making amends. It's called Karma."

"Are you Muslim?" asked Brio.

"No. My mother is, but she doesn't go to the mosque."

"And your father?"

"He grew up Catholic, but he doesn't attend church anymore."

"So, do you believe in God?"

"Yes, but I believe that we are each responsible for our own behavior and, if we do wrong, we can make it right by doing good."

"So, *you* are in control of your own little universe," concluded Brio.

As they left the gloomy church with its old moldy smell, they walked for a while in the sunshine among the shops and peeked through open doors to catch a glimpse of items being sold.

Spotting a good-looking pair of leather shoes, Richie stepped inside and examined them. However, when he was told the price, he thanked the clerk and left.

"Let's find a restaurant," Richie suggested to Brio. They chose an English pub which served a variety of beer, wine, and hard liquor. The menu was limited to a few entrees. Richie chose shepherd's pie and Brio ordered fish and chips. A couple seated at the bar were chatting with a broad London accent. (Evidently, the pub catered to tourists from England.) Richie led Brio to a quiet corner of the pub. Throughout the meal, he ignored her and conducted business or searched for information on his cell. Brio complained; Richie ignored her; Brio complained again. Suddenly, he jumped up, grabbed her by the wrist and pulled her out of the pub and up the hill. Halfway up, he dropped her wrist and left her to find her own way back to the SUV. Brio was afraid that he would leave without her. However, when she found the carpark, he was waiting by the car.

"Hurry up, selfish bitch!" he shouted.

"Don't call me a bitch! And I'm not selfish."

"Yes, you are, always wanting attention, always complaining, about the seating on the plane, about my sleeping, about my drinking, about my going out at night, about my treatment of you in bed—"

"You haven't shown any physical interest in me in Paris."

"Nor will I! You're a **liar!**"

"Liar?"

"The worst kind of liar! Making me out to be a rapist when I was feeling passionate."

"I didn't accuse you of rape."

"You went to the doctor with your so-called broken ribs. Hell, I've actually **had** broken ribs. They're fuckin' painful! "Your ribs weren't cracked, **liar!"**

"I have the x-rays at home to prove it."

"I'll bet you do. **Liar!**"

He opened the door of the car and got in. Brio quickly entered on her side; she did not want to be left to get back alone. Richie slammed the car into gear, rolled down the windows so he could smoke, turned on a hard-rock station full blast, and sped towards Paris. Brio silently endured the loud music and the cold winter air all the way home. When they arrived, he stopped in front of the hotel and yelled, **"Get out!"**

Chapter XI

Fear

Brio did not expect to see Richie again that evening, but he soon appeared with a large bottle of whiskey and two glasses. He poured a few ounces into a glass for Brio and a full glass for himself.

"You'd better drink this," he said. "I have something to say to you." Brio took a sip.

"Being together isn't going to work." Brio immediately took off her diamond and handed it to him.

"Hell, I don't want this," he said, throwing it onto the floor. "I'm going out! I'm going to listen to loud music in the SUV, drive around Paris, maybe find someone who doesn't consider me a rapist." He drained his glass and slammed out of the room.

Brio sat for a while on the bed and tried to understand his behavior. Perhaps her asking him to describe his life had dredged up memories which were too unpleasant for him to handle; or perhaps he couldn't handle the rapist charge that he thought Brio had made against him; or perhaps it was a combination of the two. Brio came to the conclusion that Richie was right.

Being together was not going to work. However, a lot of her money was tied up in business ventures with him, and she was determined to get some of it back. She sat on the bed with a pad and pen and made a list of all of the monetary expenses she had had to date on his behalf. She would hand the sheet to him when he returned – **if** he returned.

At two o'clock a.m., he stumbled through the doorway, almost falling into the room. He tore off his coat and threw it onto the floor. He walked over to Brio and shook her awake. She handed him the sheet of paper listing all of her expenditures on his behalf. He studied it for a minute and then yelled, **"You bitch!"** He tore the sheet into pieces and threw them into the air. Grabbing her by the wrist, he yanked her out of bed. She was trapped – the bed on the left, the desk on the right, and Richie in front of her. The look on his face showed him to be in a violent frame of mind, but there was no way for Brio to escape. He began hitting and slapping her, blows and slaps from left to right, back and forth, again and again until her entire face, head, neck, shoulders, and back had become a mass of inflamed and swollen flesh. Brio was in such a state of shock, she could not cry out. She could only whimper. She fell to the floor and curled up into a ball, trying to protect herself with her hands and arms. Richie became even angrier. He kicked her in the legs, the back, the ribs, and on her hands and arms. She was barely conscious when he stopped; she was shivering and shuddering uncontrollably, anticipating more blows.

Richie pulled her up and raised his hand again, but when he stared at her, he saw her black eyes and bruises beginning to darken, her swollen face and lumps forming on her head and body, and a look of fear and terror on her face.

"Oh, my God, what have I done?" he gasped. He got a glass of water for Brio from the bathroom.

"Here, Brio, sit here and drink this." She could not drink it. Her gums were bleeding, her mouth was almost swollen shut, and she was shaking too badly to hold the glass.

"Let me go to bed," she pleaded. He helped her into bed and pulled up the covers. She curled up into a fetal position on the very edge of the bed and lay as quiet as a mouse hiding from a cat. Richie turned off the light and crawled into bed with his clothes on. He lay awake all night, listening to Brio's soft sobs and wondered how he could turn this "wrong" into a "right." He remembered Brio's words, "So, you are in control of your own little universe."

Brio's fear continued the next day. She knew that she couldn't cope alone in Paris. Richie had her passport and her plane ticket, and he had the SUV. He could easily desert her and leave her to fend for herself in France, without aid or money. She decided that she would have to somehow placate Richie and encourage him to see her home to safety.

By morning, Richie had decided that in order to turn the wrong into a right, he would need to turn himself in to the French police. When he told this to Brio, she said, "No, that won't make it right. Besides, I don't want to see your life ruined." She realized that if he were taken away, she would be left alone to find a way home.

"No, Brio," he responded. "I can't live with this guilt. I need to pay for my actions."

"You can't pay for your past actions. You can only ask for forgiveness."

"You'll never forgive me for this."

"I believe in forgiveness. We all need forgiveness at times. Let's go home, Richie. You can think this through more clearly there."

"O.K., Brio. We leave tomorrow, but I think you should stay here and rest all day. I'll bring in meals and take care of the arrangements. This evening, though, we'll both have to go to a pharmacy to get our Covid tests for the flight."

"O.K. I'll feel better by then."

In the evening, when Richie and Brio left the hotel to walk to the pharmacy, Brio wore clothing to hide the bruises and lumps on her body, but her face and head looked like she had been fighting in a war. The hotel staff must have noticed her black eyes and her swollen and bruised face, but they said nothing. At the pharmacy, Brio had another shock. Richie tested negative for Covid, but she tested positive. She had contracted Covid in France! Richie showed his passport to the authority and received a certificate for travel. As he walked with Brio back to the hotel, he informed her that he had an idea of how to get her a certificate to board the plane. He escorted her to the room and then left, saying, "Wait here." Brio did as he had ordered, but she waited in fear. *Richie was free to travel; she was not. Perhaps he would leave her stranded.*

Two hours later, Richie returned with her passport and a certificate declaring her negative for Covid.

"I found a pharmacy that accepted my blood and your passport," he announced.

"How did you manage to do that?"

"I have my ways. Leave it at that. We're ready to go." Brio did not say another word about it.

Towards evening, Richie asked Brio if she felt well enough for a last visit to the Eiffel Tower. "The city lights and the fresh air would be good for us both," he said. Brio agreed and Richie walked to the garage for the SUV. He drove them to a square near the tower, where he parked the car. Gently holding Brio's hand, he guided her in the dusk towards the lights of the tower and then up the elevator. As they viewed Paris from the platform, he put his arm around Brio's shoulders. *He's trying to make amends*, she thought.

"Goodbye, Paris," Brio said as they left the tower.

"We'll come again," added Richie. "It will be better next time," he promised.

Brio thought, *it will take me a long time to recover from this time. I don't think I will ever be here again.*

The trip home was stressful. Richie did not leave early enough for the airport. At the last minute, he stopped at the bakery next to the hotel for two dozen pastries to take home to his employees. (Brio thought they would become stale, but she said nothing.) He asked the clerk to pack them into a box and tightly secure it as a carry-on package. It was still the holiday season, and traffic within Paris and on the highway leading to the airport was heavy. Richie became exasperated and burst into a stream of expletives. Brio was careful to say nothing.

They managed to return the SUV, check their bags, go through security, and walk to the gate just in time. As they entered the first-class section of the jet, Brio felt relieved. She was happy to see that they had been assigned cubicles across the aisle from each other. He could "keep an eye on her," and she could "keep two eyes on him." So far, he had treated her like a fragile package.

The six-hour flight to Atlanta gave Brio time to think about Paris. The city of "light and love" had not worked wonders for their relationship; it had been the site of a catastrophe. As a young woman, when Brio had spent a week in Paris on a study tour, Paris seemed full of light, love and wonder, but she had no lover to enjoy it with her. This time, her anticipation of romance had been replaced with fearful memories in the hotel room.

She wondered how she could have so misjudged Richie. She had always considered herself a good judge of character; she was intelligent (she could reason and come to logical conclusions); she was a mature woman, well-educated, experienced in life; she was moralistic: she had a belief in God and a firm understanding of right and wrong. On the other hand, she wondered if she deserved what had happened. Had she been vain, thinking of herself as a younger woman, still to be admired and pursued? Perhaps going to Paris with Richie had been the act of a foolish, romantic woman.

She mulled it over and concluded that her nature had played a role in the scenario of abuse. But Richie had been the **abuser,** and no woman deserved to be severely beaten! Brio decided that she would have to continue to find ways to placate him. She would try to avoid angering him by being passive. If possible, she would attempt to get some of her money back. (She had a fear of being left a pauper.) But eventually, she would leave him. Having made a plan for the future, she stretched out in her cubicle to rest peacefully for the night.

Their plane arrived late in Atlanta. After the long lines through customs, they raced to the gate for their flight to San Antonio, but the plane had just left.

"Now what?" asked Brio.

"Here, sit here with your baggage," he answered. "I'll try to get a flight to San Antonio."

Brio seated herself and changed her wrist watch to East Coast time. She was not feeling well. Her body ached all over and she had a splitting headache. She brought out her book and tried to read. After an hour, she left the baggage, walked to a restroom, and bought a packet of Mentos on the way back. She kept checking the time and watching the aisles for Richie. An hour later, she was feeling anxious and frightened again. *He must have left*, she thought; *he took his bags with him; he's deserted me. Now, how will I get home?* She looked around for an information desk, but there wasn't one in sight. She decided to ask an attendant at a nearby gate for help. Brio told the employee that she felt that she had been deserted. "Can you call a security person or someone who helps travelers?" she asked. "Look for an information desk," the attendant uncaringly answered.

Just then, Richie came in sight. He had two tickets for a flight home in two hours.

"Good," said Brio. "There's time to eat."

"I'm not hungry. You go and leave your baggage here."

Because Brio did not want him out of her sight, she did not go alone. Instead, they headed for the gate where they would board for San Antonio. It was clear across the airport, which meant long stretches of walking and going up and down escalators with their baggage. Brio suggested that they call for a cart; Richie ignored her. He impatiently walked ahead of Brio, paying no attention to her struggling. She had a fear of losing sight of him, like a child trailing her parent. The escalators were very tall and Brio was afraid of falling. She stood at the top of one, hesitant to maneuver her baggage and herself onto the moving steps. When Richie realized that she was not behind him, he angrily called up to her. "Get on! Don't be such a baby!"

"We should have called for a cart," said Brio when they reached the gate.

"You were perfectly capable of walking, Brio. Don't be a complainer." Brio was quiet. Complaining had led last time to a beating.

On the final leg of their journey, they were seated near the restroom in the back of the plane. There were three seats in the row; Richie took the window seat, and Brio sat in the middle, next to a polite female physician who did not comment on Brio's injuries. Completely ignoring Brio, Richie slept all of the way. When they arrived in San Antonio, she again trailed behind him to the baggage area for their check-on luggage and then to the garage for the Lincoln SUV.

On the drive to Brio's condo, Brio hunted for her keys. She had put them somewhere for safekeeping, but she couldn't remember where. Needing to urinate, she asked Richie to stop at a gas station.

"You can wait," he said. "We're almost there." When they pulled up to the front door, she was still searching for her keys.

"I still have to go – badly now; I'm going to wet my pants."

"For God's sake, go pee in the bushes! I'll find those damned keys."

Brio walked around to the bushes on the side of the garage and relieved herself. When she came back, Richie had the door open and all of her luggage inside the condo. *Perhaps he had my keys all along,* thought Brio. Richie left without saying goodnight – or goodbye.

Immediately upon entering, Brio called for Mickey, who came slowly down the stairs. *He has probably been asleep on my bed,* thought Brio. She picked him up and cuddled him in her arms. Then she held him aloft to look into his face. "Mickey, Mickey, Mickey, why did I want to go to Paris? I missed you, my sweet boy!" She kissed the top of his head. It was four o'clock in the morning, too late to go to bed, too early to start the new day. She carried Mickey to the couch and curled up with him. *Why are animals so good and humans so bad,* was her last thought before falling asleep.

Chapter XII

Be Mine

When Richie came four days later to see Brio at her condo, he did not mention Paris. It was as though the beating had never occurred. Instead, he was concerned about a company in Austin, who had taken civil action against B and R Home Services for unsatisfactory construction work.

A case had been opened with the district court and Brio had been listed as a defendant.

"Why me? I have not been involved in the running of the company. You have never told me about individual service contracts. I've only been an investor."

"That's it. They think you are a wealthy investor and you are listed as president of the company."

"You listed me as president?"

"I told you that, Brio." (She had no memory of being told, but Richie had accused her before of forgetting important facts, and she was afraid of arguing with him.)

"B and R is an LLC company. Isn't that protection against a lawsuit?" she asked.

"Yes, it should be. I've called a lawyer to get his advice on how to handle this."

Two days later, Richie relayed the lawyer's advice. Brio should not rely on protection from the LLC status. To be safe, she should take the title to her condo out of the family trust and put it into her name only. She could then protect the condo through the Homestead Act, which applied to people, but not to trusts. Several legal and business steps would be required to achieve this and that would take time. In the meantime, the property could be secured by temporarily selling it to Richie for ten dollars. The sale would be revoked once the new title was issued, with Brio, not the trust, as the sole owner. Brio thought that this was a convoluted arrangement, but she was now afraid of losing her main asset, her condo.

On Valentine's Day, Richie had a large bouquet of white lilies, red roses, pink mums, and sprigs of baby's breath delivered to Brio. A "romantic" message was included: *Be ready for a trip to the county clerk's office on February 17th*. However, Richie did not wait until the 17th. On the 15th, he picked her up to sign papers. Since the title had come through in her name, she could now legally protect her property. Richie relayed advice from his lawyer: A mortgage on her condo would be added protection against the plaintiffs in Austin. In the meantime, Brio should turn the mortgage amount over to Richie so that it would appear that there were very few assets left in Brio's estate. Richie would return it when the lawyer felt it was safe to do so.

Richie had once described himself as a fast mover, and Brio had just experienced a merry-go-round of events. She wondered if she should get off the merry-go-round now and take her chances alone with the lawsuit, or if she should wait until they were married, at which time she would own half of Richie's assets. However, the beating in Paris was still fresh in her mind. She was fearful of arguing with Richie, and she was worried about being left penniless. She decided that she had no choice but to sign the papers. On the 16th, Richie came to take her to the bank so that she could hand him a cashier's check for the amount of the mortgage.

Richie had invited her to his house for a steak dinner that evening. They would discuss their marriage, scheduled for the next day. At the last minute, he cancelled, and Brio ate alone at her condo. She was almost ready for bed when she heard knocking at the door. She opened it to find Richie. He said exactly what he had said in Paris, "Being together isn't going to work." Brio was not surprised; a leopard does not change his spots. "I think we should return to a strictly business relationship," he added.

"Yes, but remember, I am part owner of your companies, and I am the lender for your house. I don't think you can just walk away from your commitments."

She quickly slammed the door in his face and turned off the porch light.

"That's that," she said to Mickey. "You and I may soon be poor."

A week later, Richie called. Brio did not answer her cell; he called again; no answer. A short while later, he knocked on her door. Brio was upstairs. She peeked out the window of the guest bedroom and saw his Lincoln, but she did not go down to answer. He pounded on the door and yelled her name. She was afraid now; she was not safe upstairs; there was no escape there from an intruder. He banged and yelled again, this time loud enough to alert the neighborhood. She crept down the stairs and crouched low in the hall to enter the laundry room, an inside room. If he broke down the front door, she could quickly duck around the corner into the garage and escape in her Mini Cooper. She heard him pound on the side of the garage, close to the patio door in the kitchen. *My God,* she thought, *if he breaks in, it will be Paris all over again.*
However, the patio was surrounded by a high wall, and he did not attempt to climb it.

As soon as he left, she packed a suitcase with clothing and a satchel with toiletries, and loaded a box with her manuscript and important business and personal papers. She put Mickey into the cat carrier, gathered his supplies, and loaded everything into the Mini. If Richie returned, he could not easily see into the garage and would not know that she had left. She secured the condo and headed for a Best Western, her go-to motel for Mickey and herself.

For the next ten days, Richie called her repeatedly on her cell. She did not answer any calls at that time. She checked her messages and reviewed the telephone numbers and locations of the callers to avoid being tricked into answering.

"Well, here we are alone again, in a strange place, sleeping on a different bed," she said to Mickey. "You poor old fellow, you must be confused with what's going on." But Mickey took everything in his stride. He was a good sport, easy to please and grateful for attention. Brio alerted the motel clerks about the reason for her extended stay, and they treated her and Mickey with empathy.

Each day, her morning began with breakfast in the lobby. After morning ablutions, she read or worked on her manuscript. She left Mickey in the motel when she drove to lunch or went shopping. She napped in the afternoon and then watched news on T.V. until dinnertime, when she again left the motel. In the evening, she read or watched a movie on T.V.

"It's a quiet existence, Mickey, but a safe one." Mickey did not respond. He was taking his eighth nap of the day. On Day 10, the cell repeatedly buzzed, always with the same number, which was a local one. Brio looked through her contacts and saw that the number was from her doctor's office. Since she was expecting some test results, she answered the next time her cell buzzed. It was Richie. (He knew her doctor's number and used his cyber skills to change the source of the call.)

"Brio, don't hang up!" he said anxiously.

"How did you get me to answer?"

"I have my ways. I need to see you about the lawsuit. It's urgent!"

"I can't. It's too risky for me."

"Meet me in a public place, at Alexander's. We've been there before."

When Brio arrived at the restaurant, he was waiting in the parking lot. Brio glanced at his satchel and raised her eyebrows.

"Papers about the lawsuit," he explained.

As soon as they were seated inside the restaurant, he took out of the satchel a bouquet of red roses and a box of candy, which he handed to Brio.

"Another trick?" she asked.

"Open the lid." *It had better not be a trick,* she thought. Inside was a card with a simple message: BE MINE. "Forever," he added as he came around to her side of the booth and reached for her hand.

"Brio, I need you. As my business partner, my friend, my sister, my mother, and my wife," he implored.

"And in that order," she responded. "So, this is not about the lawsuit."

"No, it's more important than that. I've arranged for Jake and Alice to meet us tomorrow at the county clerk's office to act as witnesses to our marriage. I can't lose you, Brio."

"Nor I you," thought Brio. "If we're married, I will be entitled to everything you now have through the community property law."

"We'll do better this time," Richie promised.

"Hopefully, better and not worse," Brio responded.

After dinner and a glass of champagne together, Richie left for his home. Brio returned to the motel to pay her bill, pack, and collect Mickey.

"Let's go home, Mickey, to *our* home. No matter what happens, I promise you that *we* will stay *together, for better or for worse.*"

On March 6th, Richie called for Brio, as promised. As he drove to the county clerk's office, he informed her that Jake and Alice would not be coming. Witnesses were not needed for a marriage license, and the ceremony was merely a formality, not a requirement in Texas law. In the chamber, Brio and Richie signed the license application and took an oath to confirm that the information on the application was "the whole truth and nothing but the truth."

Brio proposed lunch to celebrate. Richie said that he had business plans; they would celebrate at a later time. He headed for Brio's condo. *Here we go again,* thought Brio. *Up, down, back and forth, ding-dong. I love you. I'm busy. I need you. Not now. Later.* She determined that she had better spend most of her time at her condo. As she left the car, she said to Richie, "I will need to spend a lot of time each day at my condo. Mickey needs care and companionship. I have mail to deal with and work to do on my computer. It will take me time to finish my manuscript."

"That's O.K. Just make sure you're at *our* house when Jena gets home from school and when I'm gone in the evening."

That's why you need me now, to babysit Jena, thought Brio.

As they began the marriage, she understood her role as Richie's wife to be two-fold: a stepmother to Jena and a housekeeper for Richie. For herself, she intended to make her role three-fold; she would also be a housekeeper for Mickey and herself. As long as she had Mickey and her condo, she could escape to think quietly and re-coop.

Chapter XIII
Living with Jena

Richie had brought Jena from Europe in mid-November and had been her sole guardian for three months. During that time, he had pampered her with a large, new wardrobe and with excursions to a theme park or to the beach. He had catered to her choice of food: Mediterranean cuisine, which she had enjoyed in Europe, and fast food (especially from McDonalds), which she enjoyed in her new country. From the grocery store, he had purchased enough snacks to fill an entire pantry. He had given her gifts of jewelry, toys, and electronic devices: a T.V., cell phone, tablet, computer, and a CD player with earphones. She had only to "ask" and she "received." He had spoiled her! Having raised children, Brio could see that Richie was making a big mistake; a sensible father did not behave this way.

Richie had allowed Jena to be lazy and sloppy. He assigned her only a few household chores: taking out the garbage and emptying the litter box. Everything else was done by the two maids, who came once a week. They did all of the laundry, tidied up the mess in the house, changed the beds, vacuumed, mopped the floors, cleaned the kitchen and the bathrooms, dusted, loaded the dishwasher, and cleared the counters of leftover food, bottles, open containers, trash, and grease and grime.

Richie had also permitted Jena to become careless in her personal habits. She never closed a cabinet door after opening it, put an item away after using it, pushed a drawer back in after obtaining an object, closed the microwave after using it, picked up clothes she had left on the floor, made her bed, replaced a cap on a bottle or a lid on a jar, or cleaned leftover food from her plate, bowl or pan. Brio had to either live with this disarray or nag Jena about it. Richie's personal habits were far from perfect, but Brio rated him a B-minus and Jena an F-minus.

Richie was lax in disciplining Jena. She was disrespectful to her elders and to the maids. If reprimanded, she made excuses for her misbehavior. Ignoring her homework, she spent too much time on her cell phone or watching T.V. She tried to make herself desirable to boys by wearing tight or skimpy clothing, fixing her hair to attract attention, applying heavy makeup, and painting her nails in bright or unusual shades. Richie did not reprimand her for sleeping too late to catch the school bus in the morning. He got up and drove her, but she often arrived too late for chemistry, her first class of the day. Ignoring dinnertime, Jena frequently disturbed the household by eating in the middle of the night. If she wanted a pastrami sandwich or noodles, she got up and fixed it. Richie had allowed her to use the kitchen whenever she wanted to and all areas of the house, with the exception of his office and the master bedroom. However, when he was not at home, she crept into these rooms anyway.

When Brio joined Richie's household part time on March 10th, she felt like a "third wheel." Richie and Jena already had an established relationship, that of a permissive father and a spoiled, self-indulgent daughter. Jena had been courteous to Brio when Brio was living primarily at her condo. But she had no intention of accepting Brio as a mother figure, counselor, teacher, or friend. The language barrier became a major problem. Richie and Jena had been conversing in Arabic, their native language, and there were no cognates between Arabic and English. As Brio stood by, listening to them as they talked, she felt ignored. If she asked them to speak in English, Richie tried to, but Jena quickly lapsed into Arabic. A repeated request from Brio brought a short translation from Richie, and Brio could tell that he had relayed only a portion of what they had been saying. Since Brio was afraid to pursue it, the problem remained unresolved.

Because Jena knew that she had the upper hand, she ignored Brio's requests to "turn off the light" or "put it into the refrigerator" or "load it into the dishwasher." If Brio tried to correct Jena's behavior, Jena often responded by sassing Brio or turning her back on her. If an argument ensued, Richie intervened and reprimanded both of them. "Jena, you are a child, but you can do better. Brio, you are the adult. Act like one."

Brio found that kind of remark degrading. She had taught her own child and hundreds of other children to be polite and respectable.

Jena was a manipulator. She could be pleasant to Brio when Richie was around and became unpleasant as soon as he left home or closed the door to his office. She was also sneaky. On one occasion, she took the key to the Mercedes and crept out for a joy ride. Furthermore, she was a flatterer. When she wanted something, she cuddled up to Richie and smothered his neck and cheeks with kisses.

As time went on, Jena isolated herself in her bedroom. There she could watch T.V., play with the cats, eat and drink, listen to music, talk on her cell phone, or communicate via her laptop. After a few weeks, Brio had her number, but it took Richie until the end of the school year to see beyond the facade.

At the beginning of May, Richie was warned by the school that Jena was failing chemistry and not doing well in many of her other classes. She had missed a majority of the class time in chemistry because she couldn't, or wouldn't, get up in the morning. Richie turned the job over to Brio: to arise early, awaken Jena and get her up, and then drive her to school. Jena never responded to Brio's first or second call. Brio needed to enter her room and pull off her covers, or wake up Richie for help. The drive to school was unpleasant because Jena was always morose.

Richie's efforts were too late. Jena would fail and have to repeat chemistry next year or go to summer school. There was only one escape. The chemistry teacher sent home a long review test, containing many different problems to solve. If Jena could do the problems, she would pass. Neither Richie nor Jena told Brio about the plan they had concocted to achieve a passing grade. Richie hired John, a tutor, to come to the house on Saturday to work with Jena. Brio heard them from the adjacent room, where she had gone to read. With each problem, John explained how to solve it, asked Jena a few questions, and then did the problem himself. They finished late in the afternoon. Several days later, the chemistry teacher informed Jena that she had passed.

It had been John's work. Brio reminded Richie and Jena that Jena had not earned a passing grade; she had not learned the material and had not done the problems. The only thing she had learned was how to be dishonest.

Summer vacation started for Jena, but it did not mean free time for her. She would still have to go to summer school to improve her grade point average. It was scheduled to start the last week in June. Richie proposed sending Jena and Brio on a cruise for a week before summer school began. He would need to stay at home to work and save money. Jena was eager to go. Brio was not; she could not see herself chaperoning Jena on a pleasure boat. Besides, Brio had already planned to visit her family in California. During the next few weeks, she wanted to spend more time with Mickey.

At the condo, Mickey became her close companion again. She felt uneasy about leaving him alone during her upcoming trip. "Well, old guy, I wish I could take you with me," she said. She knew that she couldn't; he was too old and wouldn't be able to handle the plane rides. She would hire a cat sitter to come daily to care for him. Retrieving a soft brush from the shelf of an antique table, she began brushing his fur. She noticed how matted and greasy-looking his fur was. He was extremely thin, too, with bones so prominent, she was afraid of hurting him.

"You look pretty enough, Mickey, just the way you are. But tomorrow we'll go to see the vet." She gently kissed the top of his head.

Chapter XIV

Decisions and Consequences

The exam by the vet revealed that Mickey was near death. He had advanced kidney disease and should be put out of his misery. A fatal injection would be quick, painless, and merciful. Brio agreed to take Mickey home for only a day before she brought him back, to witness his last moments.

The following day, she cuddled with him on the couch until it was time to go back to the vet. Mickey was unaware that his last car trip was about to occur. "Mickey," Brio cried as she opened the door of the cat carrier, "how can I let you go? You have been my faithful companion and comforter for so long." She lifted him up so that she could see into his eyes. He had the clouded look of a helpless, wounded creature. "It's time to let you go," she said softly, as she carefully put him into the carrier.

Brio spent a few days winding up affairs at the condo before she returned to Richie's. (He had referred to it as *our* home, but to Brio, it did not feel like home, a place where one feels contented and at ease.) She found Richie anxious and irritable. He wanted to be left alone in his office with his computer or by the pool with his cell phone. During a coffee break, she approached him.

"What's bothering you, Richie?"

"Business. Nothing you need to know." He changed the subject. "Brio, I don't want you to go to California. You should be here taking care of Jena."

"I can't be her babysitter. She doesn't want that and neither do I."

"She's just a *child*, Brio."

"Open your eyes, Richie; she's a teenager learning how to become an adult."

"I can't leave her alone while you're gone."

"She's old enough to care for herself during the day, and you can be with her at night."

"Well, have it your own way, Brio, and have a good time!" He picked up his cell phone, thus demonstrating that she had been dismissed.

For several months, Brio had been anticipating summer vacation from school, when she could be more independent. Because she had been gradually saving money from the lifetime annuity that Ben had left her, she had enough for a plane ticket and a little spending money. (When Brio and Richie were first married, he had given her $1,000 in cash and a check book with his and her names on the checks. She had used the checks for groceries until the account was dry.

When the cash was gone, Richie told her to use her own funds; he would reimburse her.) But now, she did not want him to reimburse her; the annuity allowed her a little independence. During the next week, she made her own plane reservations and connections.

The night before she left, Richie warned her not to divulge private information. He emphasized his words: "The less your family knows about **me**, the better for **you**, and the less they know about **our** finances, the better for **us**."

"Why?" asked Brio. "They have no reason to be indiscreet."

"Remember, we have a lawsuit pending. Any financial information should be given only to **our** lawyer."

Brio's flight included a brief stop at the airport in Santa Fe, allowing time for passengers to get off and other travelers to board. As the plane ascended, Brio recognized landmarks of Santa Fe and the Eldorado area where she had lived with Ben. Upon landing in Denver, she had a two-hour wait, enough time to take the train to another terminal and walk to her gate. In the plane, as she settled back in her seat with a bourbon and soda, she organized her thoughts for the visit. She would divulge some information about Jena and talk about losing Mickey. She chose selective facts to reveal about Richie, avoiding the topics of finance, threats, and abuse.

Perhaps, she would tell them about the marriage.

Lily and her husband, Sam, were there to meet her when she came down the corridor at the airport. Lily greeted her.

"Hello, Mom! You look great; still young and spry!"

"Welcome back to California!" added Sam.

Brio needed to be spry to keep up with Lily and Sam during the next week. Because they were both high school teachers and were on summer vacation, they were able to make her the center of attention. They had planned a different excursion for each day: a trip to the beach in Santa Cruz; a drive through the mountains to Big Basin to see the redwoods; a jaunt to the town of Lodi for shopping, wine-tasting, and brunch at a charming bistro; a nostalgic visit to Los Gatos, where Lily had lived with her parents until she and Sam were married.

In Los Gatos, Lily and Brio took a walking tour. They strolled by the vibrant green lawns of Los Gatos High School and past the buildings in the downtown area: the antique store that had been the Opera House in the 1800's; the old bank, with its unique outdoor-hanging clock; the brick corner drugstore, with its old-fashioned turret. Across the street was a park with a fountain and tall redwoods. A view of the nearby foothills reminded Brio that she and Ben had been daily surrounded by this charm and beauty and had chosen to leave it all behind.

For the final day of Brio's stay, Lily and Sam hosted a sit-down dinner, with the whole family present. The grandchildren (Carla, Melanie, and Jamie) were inquisitive about Brio's life in Texas. As planned, Brio was careful not to open *Pandora's box.* However, towards the end of the meal, she relayed that she and Richie had been married in March. Everyone sat like statues. Sam broke the silence. "Why didn't you tell us?" he asked.

"I wanted to tell all of you in person when we were together."

Carla left the table and walked into the hall; Melanie busied herself by carrying dishes into the kitchen. Jamie showed no reaction. Lily finally spoke. "It will take some time to get used to him. He's so different from Dad."

Well, that's done, thought Brio. *Where do I go from here?*

Chapter XV

Return to San Antonio

When Brio arrived at the airport in San Antonio, she expected to see Alfie, one of Richie's employees, who was supposed to drive her home. He was late. Brio collected her luggage and seated herself on a bench where she could watch the doors to the baggage area, as well as the carousel. After several hours, she considered taking a taxi home, but it was too late. The taxi drivers had already gone. About 3:00 p.m., Alfie arrived.

"It's too late to go to Richie's house," said Brio. "The night is half over and I don't want to wake up Jena. So, just take me to my condo."

When she entered the hall, she momentarily expected Mickey to greet her, but then she remembered. She quickly changed into her pajamas and climbed into bed at 4:00 p.m.

She awakened at noon, brushed her teeth, and combed her hair. She planned to come back later, after she had checked on Jena. When Brio arrived at Richie's, Jena was still asleep. Brio knocked on her bedroom door, but she got no response. She checked the house. The cats were on the sofa; the lights were on; leftover food sat on the counter; the door to the pool was unlocked. Brio took a drink and her book and went out by the pool. Through the window, she saw Jena come into the kitchen to get food and a drink to take upstairs. *Jena must be avoiding me*, Brio thought. Around 6:00 p.m., Brio knocked on Jena's door and said, "I'm going to McDonald's (Jena's favorite place). Want to come?"

"No," she mumbled.

"Well, I need to go back to my condo, Jena. I'm expecting a call on the landline from my daughter." Jena did not respond.

Later that day, Brio was reluctant to return to a closed door and a sixteen-year-old who was petulant and behaving like a two-year-old. Brio remembered herself at sixteen: a good student and a skilled and disciplined musician who had already graduated from a music conservatory. Surely, Jena should be capable of sleeping through the night without *mommy bringing her a bottle*. However, Brio dutifully moved back to "chaperone" the cats and Jena, who continued to isolate herself.

When Richie came home six days later, Jena was still in her room.

"How's Jena?" he asked.

"Fine, I guess. She's confined herself to her room. My goodness! You look like you've been on an ocean cruise! Where did you get that tan? I thought that military installations were usually underground."

"They are, but occasionally I have to go up to the roof to work on cables," he answered good-naturedly.

When Richie's tan wore off, his good spirits turned to gloom. He was irritable, anxious, and preoccupied. Eventually, he appealed to Brio for help. He was strapped for money. If Brio sold her condo, it would help them both. They would no longer have a costly monthly mortgage payment, the monthly HOA fees, insurance, taxes, and utility bills for the condo.

"You don't have to have two places to stay," he said to Brio. "Your place is here with me and Jena." *He's right*, Brio thought. *I can barely afford my condo, especially if I have to help with the grocery and liquor bills. Besides, Mickey is gone now*. When Brio agreed to sell the condo, Richie moved quickly. He engaged his friend, Hannah, to list the condo at a price that Brio considered too high, but she signed the agreement on July 2nd, with the assurance that she could keep her baby grand piano, along with many of her beautiful Persian rugs, paintings, and antique furniture.

Richie found a storage place and hired movers to take the less expensive furniture, rugs, and belongings to a unit there. A week later, he suggested that the movers bring some of the expensive pieces to their home; the living room was empty and Brio could arrange them there.

Brio again agreed, and the second lot was moved. When a third lot was proposed, Brio refused. Until the condo sold, she wanted to retain enough furniture and works of art to have a lovely and peaceful place for refuge.

An argument started in the living room of the condo. Richie and Brio went around and around in circles. The condo, according to Richie, needed to sell quickly at a high price. Hannah knew best how to make that happen. Sparsely furnished condos allowed a buyer to visualize the rooms with their furniture in it. Hannah suggested that only choice items should stay: in the living room, the baby grand; in the guest bedroom, the four-poster bed; in the computer room, a leather chair and ottoman, the desk and chair, a table, and a standing lamp. Hannah would bring in a few other pieces to stage the rooms tastefully. *Huh*, thought Brio. *So, I have no taste in decorating.* Her feelings were hurt, and she was fed up with being pushed around by Hannah and Richie. As they argued, Brio became more upset and animated. Finally, Richie said, "I'm not afraid of you, Brio. Let's go home. I'll put steaks on the grill." Brio was happy that she had won the argument, but she wondered about his using the word "afraid."

Brio and Richie seemed to be enjoying the evening. The steaks were good; the wine was relaxing; the lights on the pool were soft and soothing. Suddenly, Richie's cell phone disrupted the peace. "I have to go," he relayed. "One of my employees needs my help."

It was three hours before Richie returned. Brio had stayed up to wait for him.

"Well, Brio," he said, smiling, "you can't go back to your condo again. It's now staged as Hannah wants it."

"Where are my things?"

"The furniture is in the garage. The mirrors and rugs are in the closets. The paintings are under the four-poster bed. Hannah and I moved everything ourselves." Brio said nothing.

"So, you can't go back, Brio."

No, she thought, *nor can I stay here. What a dirty trick to play on me!*

Brio settled in to a life akin to a cross between a vegetable and a rabbit. She was afraid and alert, and she had to remain quiet. One morning, as usual, she tidied up the master bedroom before joining Richie on the patio for coffee. She made the bed, picked up the clothes he had left on the floor the previous night, put away his slippers, hung his towel up neatly, and closed the drawers he had left open – all except one. Something in the drawer attracted her attention. As soon as she began reading the document, she understood why Richie had acquired the deep tan he had when she returned from California. The document was a two-page listing of all charges for Mr. Richie Campianno and Mrs. Gabriela Bezique, with Mr. Campianno as the responsible party. Both parties had shared the same cabin on a Carnival cruise, with the sale date 06/18/2022. Brio reasoned that they must have left for the trip on the day before she returned from California, perhaps staying overnight in the port city for an early-morning departure.

The list of charges included numerous drinks at various bars on the ship: the Burgundy Bar, the Ocean Plaza Bar, the Casino Bar, the Red Frog Rum Bar, the Pool Bar, the Lobby Bar, the Crimson UL SVC Bar, the Disco Bar, the Dining Room Bar, the Piano Bar, and the Alchemy Bar.

Good heavens! thought Brio. *They must have been drunk for the entire week!* Evidently, they had visited Cloud 9 Spa three times for a cost of $1,352.00 each. Food expenses included meals in the dining room and food delivery to their cabin. One shore excursion cost $409.00 each. Richie had charged $387.00 for gratuities, evidently trying to impress Gabriela as a big, generous spender.

Brio was disgusted with what she saw. Richie had lately been strapped for money, always asking her for more, and she had caught him on an expensive pleasure spree. He had lied to her about working hard and depriving himself while Brio took a vacation. She contemplated whether or not she should confront Richie, and she decided that she would postpone taking action until a time when it would have the greatest impact. Two could play *the deceit game*.

A short while later, Brio was tempted to confront him. He had been questioned by the Child Protection Agency about his whereabouts on June 17th and 18th. He stated that his work had taken him away from home and he had left Jena in his wife's care. The agent informed him that Jena had had an unsupervised party while he was gone. A father of one of the boys at the party had called to report the lack of parental care. From his son, he had learned that there had been drinking, marijuana smoking, and wild behavior at the pool. One of the boys had stayed overnight with Jena. The agent warned Richie that they would be checking from time to time to see that Jena was receiving proper care from an adult. In the meantime, Jena was to be supervised twenty-four hours a day by Richie.

As soon as the agent left, Richie turned on Brio. "I left her in your care and look what happened. You went off to your condo to be alone, and I'm left with a charge of child neglect. You know, a person can end up in prison for child neglect, Brio. I covered for you. **You** were the one who neglected her and I'm not willing to go to prison for you." Brio stayed as quiet as a rabbit listening for a predator. *Now is not the right time to confront him about the cruise*, she thought.
She could wait.

Richie did not know when the agency would come to check, but he wanted Jena to be able to report that he was taking good care of her; so, he began spending more time with her. Some days, he took her to work with him. She pulled cables or did simple tasks at the computer. When he needed to do an installation at a military base, he brought her along to go swimming at the pool. At home, too, he spent time with her, playing ball or goofing around in the pool.

One afternoon, Brio sat on the wicker couch, watching them. She was in a pensive mood.

"Come into the pool, sourpuss," yelled Richie. "Come on, come into the pool." She shook her head. "Not today." Richie climbed out of the pool and toweled off.

"I want to show you something," he said, reaching for her hand. She got up and went with him. When they reached the pool, he dropped her hand and pushed her into the pool. Jena thought it was uproariously funny. Brio swam to the shallow end and walked into the house without saying a word. However, she was thinking, *another dirty trick.*

Richie's days of being a better father were numbered. Jena didn't miraculously turn into a sweet, loving child. She continued lying, cheating, and deceiving. One night, Brio awakened and saw Jena creeping into the bathroom. The next morning, Brio checked her purse and found twenty dollars missing. A short while later, she saw Jena looking through Richie's desk. When Richie told Brio that he was missing a few of the marked bills that he had been keeping for a client, she relayed that she had seen Jena entering the room. Richie confronted Jena, but she claimed that she always asked when she needed money. Brio became more vigilant. One night, she was sure that she had heard the kitchen door opening and closing. She wondered if there had been an intruder in the house. "Not likely," said Richie. "Security cameras are everywhere and alarms are set to go off." Brio suggested that he review the camera footage.

After he had studied the footage, he asked Jena and Brio to come into the master bedroom. He directed Jena to sit on the bed. He closed the door to the room and sat down facing her. Brio remained standing. "You've been sneaking out at night," he said to Jena. She denied it. "Now come clean or I'll get the strap." (Richie would have made an excellent investigator; he knew how to extract information to glean the truth from the lies.)

Jena admitted that she had been stealing liquor from Richie's supply and sneaking out of the house through the kitchen door after Richie and Brio were asleep. Sometimes, she took the keys to Brio's Mini. Sometimes, she used the opener to get out of the gate and walked to a meeting spot. Richie pressed her to find out where she went and whom she met. She usually went to the gas station on the corner to meet a guy who sold her marijuana. She didn't know his name.

"How long have you been smoking marijuana?" Richie asked.

"Several months. **You** smoke it," she answered.

"I'm an adult; you're a child."

He lectured her about the seriousness of her actions. "If the Child Protection Agency finds out about this, I could go to prison." He turned to Brio. "See what happened when I was gone?" Brio said nothing. She thought, *now is not the time to confront him.*

Jena had confessed. She thought that the worst was over. "Leave us," Richie ordered Brio. He closed the door after her. Brio went downstairs. Suddenly, she heard the sound of terrified screaming, scuffling, doors banging open and shut, sobbing, and then silence. Richie had beaten Jena with his leather belt. Just listening to Jena's screams ignited Brio's own fear. *If he could do that to Jena, who was in his care---.* She fled into the backyard, into the sunshine and the sound of twittering birds.

The next day, Richie drove Jena to the airport and sent her back to Europe. He had called his parents and had told them the whole story. He relayed to Brio his final words to them: "Jena will be lost if she stays in America. We should have been better parents."

One evening, a week later, as Brio and Richie sat by the pool, Richie said, "I'm thinking of going back to Geneva. I might take you with me, Brio."

"Why Geneva?"

"I was happy at the United Nations."

"It's a beautiful area," said Brio. "I was there on a study tour of Europe after I graduated from the University of Nebraska. The grounds were beautiful, with spacious lawns around the UN building, tall cedar trees from Lebanon, flags of the different nations flying on flagpoles, and a beautiful garden with a huge golden ball, depicting the world."

"Yes, it was a pleasant place to work."

"What was your job?" asked Brio.

"I started out as a clerk. I was in charge of seeing that shipments reached their destination on time. One day, I was called into my boss's office and reprimanded for a shipment being late. Sitting in the corner of the room was a man who was not introduced to me. However, he liked the way I handled myself with diplomacy, and he called me to come to his office for an interview with him. He happened to be the Inspector General of the United Nations."

"An important man," commented Brio.

"Yes, I was suddenly promoted from a clerk to Assistant to the Inspector General."

"What a break! What was your job as his assistant?"

"A lot of the time, I was his *attaché* when he traveled throughout Europe to solve problems."

"Any memorable occasions?"

"Yes. In England we were invited to a garden party, along with hundreds of other people. We were introduced to Queen Elizabeth and Prince Philip."

"What was your impression of them?"

"Prince Philip was friendly and happy to greet us; Queen Elizabeth was cold."

"How long were you in that position?"

"Not long. Three years. I was invited to become an agent in Homeland Security in the U.S."

"So, you went from being a diplomat at the UN to a cybersecurity agent for the U.S. government."

"From a position of respect to chasing *bad guys,*" he added.

Well, he opened up a little this evening, Brio thought as she lay in bed. However, she wasn't sure that she believed everything he had told her.

Richie's communication with her did not last. The next day he was angry, withdrawn, and edgy, in a mood to criticize and reopen old wounds. They were starting the day by the pool, Brio sipping her coffee, Richie smoking and talking on his cell. After a long conversation with his mother, Richie said, "That was about Jena."

"How is she doing?"

"Not adjusting well. She really thought that she was here to stay."

"She got into bad ways."

"And that was largely **your** fault, Brio."

"And you had no role in that," she answered sarcastically.

"Jena was just a child, Brio."

"A very willful, stubborn, deceitful child. I guess deceit runs in your family."

Richie leaned forward, a question and a frown on his face.

"**Admit** it, Richie! **You** left her! **You** sneaked off for a pleasure boat cruise with Gabriela." His eyes opened wide.

"I have the proof of your drunken Carnival cruise and of the money, **our** money, you spent on liquor, spas and excursions—" Richie jumped up, grasped her wrists, and pulled her up. She pulled back, but he was too strong for her. He dragged her to the pool, picked her up, and violently threw her into the pool. Without a backward glance, he stormed into the kitchen. Brio swam from the deep to the shallow end. As she climbed out of the pool, she was aware of the pain in her lower left leg. She stood for a minute, shivering in shock. Her leg had been slammed into the cement coping around the pool. Creeping into the kitchen, she listened for sounds of movement. The house was quiet; Richie had left. He would not be back for a while. *I have a little time to pack and escape*, she reasoned.

Chapter XVI

Escape

Feeling shaken, confused, and anxious, Brio began her helter-skelter journey to Omaha, where she would seek help from her niece Maggie, who was a caregiver. Because Brio didn't have an AAA road map in the car, she set her GPS system for Santa Fe, New Mexico, which was north of San Antonio. That was the right direction to travel. The GPS led her northwest on Highway 10 towards Boerne. At the tiny village of Comfort, she turned onto 87 North to Fredericksburg. This was the same route that she had taken at an earlier, happier time with Richie. After Fredericksburg, the highway turned west towards San Angelo and Big Spring, a town with a population of 28,000. When she stopped for gas, her left leg was throbbing painfully. Her foot and leg were swollen, and a lump the size of a goose egg was forming. *No wonder it's throbbing*, she thought. *I'd better get off it for the night.*

The next morning, she drove to the town's only hospital to have her leg examined by a doctor. X-rays showed no fractures, but the extensive bruising, swelling, and pain indicated possible complications.

"Keep your leg wrapped until the swelling goes down and keep it elevated," advised the doctor. Brio said to herself, *a little difficult to do while driving*. When the doctor learned that the injury had come from abuse, he summoned a detective, who recorded the facts about the incident. However, San Antonio was not in his jurisdiction; Brio would have to return there to seek help. *Ridiculous,* she thought. *It makes no sense for an abused to return to the vicinity of the abuser.*

When Brio left Big Spring in the early afternoon, she reset the GPS for Omaha, which directed her on Highway 20 East towards Abilene, Texas. "Oh, my God," Brio muttered. "I've been going west instead of east." (She wouldn't have made the mistake if she had had a large AAA map to show her that Eastern Nebraska was both north and east of Central Texas.) *I'll have to watch the sun's position in the sky for guidance; I can't rely on the GPS*, she concluded.

From Abilene, the GPS led her north towards Wichita Falls, Texas, the last major city before she crossed the border into Oklahoma. *What route should I take in Oklahoma*, she wondered. The GPS kept trying to direct her through the largest cities of Oklahoma City and Tulsa, but Brio wanted to avoid heavy traffic. She chose Highway 81 North, the major north/south highway that would lead her eventually to her hometown of Norfolk, Nebraska. Throughout Oklahoma, she ignored the GPS and crossed the border into Kansas, stopping at Wichita for the night. As she settled down to sleep, her thoughts were whirling in a fog of exhaustion.

The Midwest goes on for miles and miles; ranchland, farmland, an occasional town; from Wichita, Texas through Oklahoma to Wichita, Kansas. - Has Richie missed me yet? She wondered.

On the third day, Brio stayed on Highway 81 North through Kansas and into Nebraska. If she had continued north, she would have reached her hometown of Norfolk, but her parents were deceased; so, she headed east to Omaha and Maggie, her niece.

Maggie was aghast when she examined Brio's leg. It was bruised from mid-calf to the bottom of her foot. Next to the bone, the lump had grown from the size of a goose egg to the size of a large potato.

"That bastard!" exclaimed Maggie. "I'm taking you to the hospital right now!"

"O.K. The little hospital in Big Spring didn't seem to know what to do for me."

Maggie drove Brio to a large hospital complex, equipped to handle all areas of medical and psychiatric cases. Brio was examined by a number of different doctors and had extensive x-rays performed. Their medical conclusion was that the bone had not been fractured but had been damaged enough for the blood to seep out of the bone and into surrounding tissue, causing the huge lump and extensive bruising. It had been a severe blow! They removed the elastic bandage because continued pressure on the wound was not helpful at this point.

When Maggie reported that her aunt had received both physical and mental abuse, Brio was questioned by a psychologist and a counselor connected with elder abuse. Then a detective was brought in to ask detailed questions. He relayed that San Antonio was not in his jurisdiction, but he would contact the San Antonio Police and send them a report, along with the medical records from the hospital.

After being questioned for several hours, Brio felt exhausted. One question had led to another. She felt like a suspected criminal in an investigation. She had been protecting herself by keeping secret the nature of her relationship with Richie. Although she was now free to talk about him, she felt uneasy because he was not there to defend himself.

On the way back to the motel, Maggie said, "Richie is an **evil** man."

"Some of his actions were evil, and he has trouble controlling himself, but I don't think he is evil," Brio responded.

"Be logical, Aunt Brio. Look how he led and manipulated you step by step."

During the week, Brio rested and recuperated. She had to determine the direction of her future. She was confused, and her thoughts bounced back and forth between memories of the "good Richie" and those of the "bad Richie."

The "good Richie" kept trying to reach her on her cell phone, but Brio wouldn't answer it. By the end of the week, she answered. She decided that he should know how badly he had hurt her. With the camera on her cell phone, she showed him the injury to her leg. Richie was dismayed and begged her to forgive him.

"Come home," he implored. "I miss you. I need you. Maya and Basha miss you."

"Remember what you said to me several times. It isn't going to work. Too much water has flowed under the bridge."

"Come back, Brio," he begged. "We'll work out our business and marital problems together."

"Together? You're a loner. You once told me that you're happiest when you are alone."

"Well, I'm not."

"I'm afraid of your temper. Remember Paris."

"What happened in Paris will never happen again. I was stinking drunk."

"And you could get that way again."

"I won't. I'll get counseling if I need it."

"You **need it**, Richie**.**"

"All right, Brio. I will. Just give me a chance." Brio promised to think about it.

In the motel room that night, Brio took a piece of hotel stationery and made a list of Richie's good and bad traits, as well as her own. The list of bad traits for Richie included self-indulgence, manipulation, aggression, secrecy, impulsiveness, and abuse. At times, his good traits were generosity, politeness, perseverance, and passion. A list of Brio's bad traits included pride, naivete, and gullibility. Her good traits were determination, creativity, empathy, and forgiveness. After studying her lists, she determined that some traits had been more destructive to their relationship than others. Richie had damaged their relationship the most by being abusive. She wondered if this abusive trait *could be overcome*, and if she *could forgive him* again. (She knew that she had needed forgiveness many times for her own misdeeds.)

When Richie called the next day, she discussed the lists she had drawn up and demanded a promise from him. "I will only return if you promise to have regular sessions with a psychiatrist," she said.

"I have a lot of changes I need to make," he admitted. "I promise to seek help."

"O.K. I'll be there in three days. In the meantime, think about turning your life around."

"Yes. I promise. Thanks, Brio. Drive carefully."

Brio invited Maggie and her twelve-year-old daughter, Sylvia, to have dinner with her at the pub. When Brio told them that she planned to go back to Richie, they looked at each other in shock.

"Don't do it, Aunt Brio," cautioned Maggie. "It wouldn't be safe. You shouldn't trust him. Remember what happened in Paris."

"I painted a very bad picture of him. I can't just walk away from a marriage."

"You already did."

"I was afraid of him."

"And rightly so. He is a classic example of a scam artist. Aunt Brio, the world is full of men like   him. He has been preying on you."

"You really think so?"

"Yes. Scammers are deceptive. They often parade as victims of abuse themselves. Many have had difficult childhoods and feel that they are entitled to take whatever they can get. Think about the money you've lost."

"I know." Brio turned to Sylvia. "What do you think?"

"I agree with Mom. You wouldn't be safe. This is the third time he has hurt you, Aunt Brio. Next time he could kill you."

When Maggie and Sylvia walked Brio back to the motel, Brio said, "I'm leaving tomorrow."

"Not for Texas, I hope."

"I don't know. I've been at a crossroads at other times in my life, and I've always been able to choose the right path forward, but this time, there is no clear way. As Scarlett O'Hara said in *Gone with the Wind*, 'I'll think about that tomorrow.'"

When *tomorrow* came, Brio called Maggie to say goodbye. "Pray for me," she said. "I've decided to drive west towards California. When I get to Colorado, I'll have to decide whether to turn south towards Texas or continue west towards California."

Chapter XVII
Finding a Way

Brio left Omaha on I-80 West, which would take her across Nebraska. Once she had left the heavy traffic of Omaha behind, her mind was free to search for the right path forward. If she never returned to San Antonio, she would be leaving all of her possessions in Richie's hands. That was unthinkable. To live without the beauty and enjoyment of art, music, and family mementos would be bleak. On the other hand, if she returned, she could lose her life. Was she willing to take that chance? Maggie and Sylvia had been fearful for her. By the time Brio reached Ogallala, which was near to the intersection of Nebraska, Wyoming, and Colorado, she was too exhausted to make the decision. She decided to rest and pray about it and, hopefully, awaken refreshed and assured of the right path.

The next day, instead of taking Highway 385 South through Colorado, New Mexico, and into Texas, she headed West on I-80 through Wyoming, Utah, and Nevada into California. If she stayed on I-80 West, it would take her all the way there. There would be places of interest along her route, but she could afford neither the time nor the money for sightseeing. Still, there was plenty to see from the car or during a brief stop. In Cheyenne, Wyoming, she stopped long enough to peek into Frontier Days of the Old West. Leaving the museum twenty minutes later, she traveled through long stretches of sagebrush-covered plains, which gradually turned into canyons, bluffs, and high plateaus. By the time she had reached the Bear River Valley, she had climbed to a peak of 6,749' and then descended to Evanston, a beautiful spot nestled in the foothills of the mountains.

As she entered Utah the next morning, she skirted around Salt Lake City to save time and "traffic nerves." After she had left the suburbs behind, she drove past the southern tip of the Great Salt Lake. Eight distant mountain ranges added beauty to the dull white wasteland of the dried salt beds. For sixty miles, Highway I-80 continued through the salt desert, which never seemed to end. *It must have been a huge lake at one time,* Brio thought, *perhaps larger than any of the Great Lakes.*

Across the border in Nevada, Highway I-80 wound through sagebrush terrain, with an occasional salt bed to break up the monotony of the desert. Three small towns (Elko, Battle Mountain, and Winnemucca) were oases for motorists needing gas, food, or water. Brio stopped for the night in Reno, Nevada, but had no interest in gambling. It had been a tedious day, and she needed to rest and think more clearly. The last time that she had been with her family, she had pretended that her marriage with Richie was a happy one. Now she dreaded the explanations of the past that lay ahead of her.

The next morning, she still felt worried as she headed for Sacramento, which was only seventy miles from her family in Manteca. She did not set her GPS because she knew the territory well. To get to the Sacramento Valley, she had to travel across the Sierra Nevada Mountains. She had often traversed these mountains with her husband Ben when he accompanied her to Reno to give an organ concert at Trinity Episcopal Cathedral. The drive had always been an exquisitely beautiful one, but an intensely nerve-wracking one. This time, Brio was alone, traveling alongside California drivers, who could be impatient and reckless.

At first, the scenery was beautiful: giant sequoias, granite cliffs, small glacial lakes, and canyons with streams. When she reached the summit, she suddenly became a bundle of nerves. The highway plunged snake-like downward from an altitude of 7,085' to 1,100' at Auburn, where it continued through gentle, rolling foothills. However, the calm of the hills was short-lived. The traffic in Sacramento was hectic, with drivers changing lanes to get to their exits. *The civil engineers for this highway must have considered cost rather than safety*, thought Brio.

When she reached Manteca, she was in a piteous state. She had the appearance of a bedraggled and injured pet who has just struggled to find its way home. Lily and Sam knew approximately when she would arrive, and they had a bedroom and a bathroom ready for her. They were aghast at Brio's injuries, but they did not press her for an explanation. "Let's get you into bed now, Mom," said Lily. "The family will be here tomorrow, and we'll all listen to your story at the same time so that you won't have to repeat it."

Before Brio began her narrative the following day, Lily informed her that she, Sam, and Carla had become suspicious and had researched Richie to the extent they could on the internet. Brio told her story chronologically, trying her best in her frazzled state to be lucid. Upon hearing the complicated story, the family members were convinced that Brio had been scammed by Richie.

Richie had met her when she was a perfect target for a confidence/romance scam. She was a widow who needed technical support, protection, and friendship. Posing as a cyber security expert, he gained control of her computer and personal financial records.

Selling her a new, overpriced computer, a surround sound system, and a home security system was just the beginning of the loss of her "nest egg." Wooing her with expensive gifts and trips, he had tricked her into thinking that he was a wealthy man who was searching for the right partner. Investment scams ensued: a loan to him for the money to buy his house, a request for "seed money" to start a new business, and requests for business expenses relating to his established business.

He often manipulated her by evoking sympathy: his poor, neglected niece needed care; he was overwhelmed by employee and financial problems; he was exhausted and working night and day; his former wife was refusing to cooperate; he had been in the hospital for illness or because of various accidents. (Sam commented, "Either he is the unluckiest man on earth or he is a liar.")

When Richie needed more control of Brio, he wooed her with a marriage proposal; he convinced her that an official ceremony was not needed. Signing a license at the county clerk's office was enough for a marriage in Texas. By community law, Brio would own half of his property, making her a wealthy widow if he died. After they were "married," he encouraged her to give him "power of attorney" so that he could transact business for **them**. They needed, he said, the equity in her condo to keep alive **their** businesses during a time of economic hardship. He encouraged her to mortgage her condo and to give him the cash for **their** business. Following the mortgage, he had put her condo up for sale.

Sam warned Brio, "There is still money he is attempting to make. When the condo sells, he will try to take the proceeds after the mortgage is paid off."

"Be careful, Grammie," said Melanie.

"I wanted to warn you against him," said Carla. "I found out plenty from the internet and from phone calls I made."

"Grammie wouldn't have listened at that time," said Lily to Carla.

"Remember, Grammie, when I started to investigate his company and him, he warned you that I had put him in danger," said Melanie to Brio.

"He changed the name of the company," said Carla.

"A typical trick by scammers," said Sam. "They begin by changing the name of a respectable company just slightly to start their own company. The customer often does not notice the difference." Brio shook her head and then sat still, like a child about to be reprimanded.

The family sat quietly, each one wondering how to proceed. Brio was thinking: *In hindsight, Richie appears only calculating, manipulative, and selfish; in reality, he was at times generous and caring. I was kept confused.*

"I wish you had let us help you, Mom," said Lily.

"I wish I had not been so trusting and naïve," responded Brio.

Sam commented, "Honest people are always easier to dupe. Scammers are good at sprinkling the truth into a batch of lies. That's what makes them so plausible."

"Yes," agreed Brio. "I'm sure that his background story was partly true. He said that he had worked at the UN and had come to Washington, D.C. before being relocated to San Antonio. His descriptions about his former life in the Mideast were full of details. They paint a picture of a disturbed youth."

"Did you love him?" asked Lily.

"Love? Perhaps. At first, I found him attractive, smart, and fun to be with. Then he became busy, and I was lobbed back and forth between loneliness and companionship. To myself, I made excuses for him. He was working hard or was away on stressful business trips. He convinced me that he needed me to take care of him and to be a mother to Jena.

"Then Paris happened and I had a shocking wake-up call. After the beating, I never trusted him again. I was afraid of what he might do if he fell into a rage or became 'stinking drunk.' I started escaping to my condo when he became depressed that business was not going well, and I was afraid that his temper would explode. Alone, I tried to think about how I could get some of my money back. Then I came to California for a visit. After my return, I discovered that he had taken a cruise with another woman. At the same time, he blamed me for leaving Jena alone. I was both hurt and angry.

"During the final months with him, I secretly started putting a plan for escape into action. I set up checking and savings accounts in another bank and began depositing my social security checks in it. (He didn't notice.) I stored important documents and personal papers in the Mini, and I kept plenty of cash on hand in case I had the opportunity to leave quickly. When he beat Jena and sent her back to Europe, I knew that I had to get out of there soon. The day that he slammed me into the pool and injured my leg, I took my chance to escape and was gone within an hour."

"You were brave," said Lily, "but you look exhausted now. Why don't you go upstairs for a nap? When you come down, we'll have supper."

Brio could tell that her family had discussed her while she had been napping because they explained ways to help her to get back on her feet. Sam would help her to maneuver her way through the sale of her condo and research ways for her to manage on a limited budget. Carla would continue monitoring the internet for business and legal information and would search for an apartment that Brio could afford. Lily would reach out to Adult Protective Services for guidance. Melanie would provide social contact to help Brio to adjust. Jamie would check daily on Brio's safety.

Near bedtime, when the house was quiet, Lily sat at the kitchen table as she corrected compositions. Brio checked her cell phone to see if Richie had left any messages. There were five voicemails:

8/18/22 @ 9:03 a.m. – "Hey, good morning. I was just joking when I threw you into the pool. It was a hot day and you needed some refreshing. So, are you going to stay mad or what? Bye."

8/18/22 @ 9:50 a.m. – "Hey, Brio, I was wondering if you would like to be present moving your stuff out or should I just go ahead and move it into storage. If

I don't receive a call from you by tomorrow, I'm going to go ahead and move it. Bye."

8/23/22 @ 10:15 a.m. – "Brio, how are you doing? I just want to make sure that you are O.K. You were supposed to come last night and you did not. I don't want to bother you if you need some time to yourself. I just want to know if you are O.K. Bye."

8/23/22 @ 11:02 a.m. – "Hey, Brio, you are really making me worry about you. Please give me a call or text me. I don't know if you've had an accident or if you're alive. You should have been here last night. I'm going to call the police for the records. Please just let me know if you're O.K. so I don't have to call the police. Bye."

8/23/22 @ 5:25 p.m. – "Hey, Brio, I think I know you are safe, and you're just trying to do whatever in not answering me. I'm going to move your furniture tomorrow to storage. It's cramped in that room with all the boxes. If you're ever going to come back, let me know or otherwise, just let me deal with those things. Bye."

Lily had been listening to the messages. She commented, "Just having fun in the pool, huh?"

"Yeah. It was a riot!" Brio answered.

"He won't call the police, Mom."

"No, he wouldn't want to be on their radar."

Chapter XVIII

Determination

During September and October, Brio lived with Sam and Lily. Her problems were not yet over. She suspected that Hannah, the realtor, was still taking orders from Richie. Unpaid mortgage payments were adding up; Brio's credit rating was being destroyed. She feared that the mortgage company would maneuver to sell the condo themselves. Hannah refused to lower the price of the condo to a reasonable one, and she failed to put it on multiple listing (evidently trying to earn the 30% seller's commission herself instead of sharing it with other realtors). Brio worried that her baby grand, oil paintings, and other valuable belongings were not safe.

In Stockton, Carla had found her a studio apartment that she could afford. It was very small, but the complex had spacious common rooms. The location was beautiful. On one side of a wide boulevard, redwood trees lined a walkway which led past a lake; on the opposite side of the boulevard, another walkway continued along expensive houses and overlooked a second lake. Several benches provided places to sit and watch the ducks, herons, egrets, and geese.

Brio drove to the apartment with a measuring tape and a notepad to determine how many pieces of furniture and oil paintings she should bring from Texas to furnish the apartment. She would be strapped for money, but she would have beautiful things about her. However, to collect her cherished belongings, she would have to return to San Antonio.

The plan she worked out was to drive to San Antonio and live for a week in a motel. During this time, she could make arrangements for moving her possessions and emptying the condo for a prospective buyer to move in. There were several steps involved:

1. Get bids on services needed.

2. Sell the baby grand, rugs, and paintings on consignment.

3. Hire a moving van to load up the items she wanted to keep.

4. Pack pieces of chinaware, personal items, and clothing into boxes; move them into the Mini.

5. Hire "Got Junk" to transport any remaining items of value to a charity and to clean out the condo.

However, when she revealed her plan to Sam and Lily, they argued against it. They had furniture in their garage that she could have. The trip back to San Antonio would be costly and stressful. Brio countered, "I don't see myself capable of happiness, living in bleak surroundings. I've lost my *nest egg*. Do I have to give up everything?" Sam and Lily went out for dinner and a movie, leaving Brio alone. The next day, Lily explained that they wanted to see her happy, but that it would be too risky for her to return to San Antonio.

Brio thought it through and devised a plan for her safety. She would live in a motel and no one need know that she was in San Antonio. Since Hannah had not been keeping in touch, it was unlikely that Brio would see her. Richie thought that she was out of the state. From the motel, she could use her laptop and her cell to make all of the arrangements for the move. When all of the details had been worked out, she would need to be at the condo for only short periods of time and there would be workers about. As for travel to and from San Antonio, she had already driven 5,000 miles alone this summer; she could manage 2,000 more. Lily and Sam were reluctant to let her embark on another trip, but they knew that she was a woman of determination.

Brio decided to take routes along the way that would be interesting. From Manteca, she chose Highway 5 South, which led past hillsides covered with golden brown grasslands and fields of orchards. As she headed for Santa Clarita, she drove through the foothills of the Tehachapi Mountains, which were carpeted with native grass that looked like golden velvet. To avoid the Los Angeles traffic, she skirted the picturesque mountain ski areas leading to Palm Springs and took the northerly route of the Joshua Tree wilderness, which continued until she reached Parker, Arizona. She stopped there for the night. To avoid the sweltering heat, she planned to enter the Sonoran Desert, the hottest desert in the United States, early in the morning.

Soon after she entered the desert, saguaro cacti began to appear. Brio had once studied about these giants: *The organ pipe saguaros can reach a height of seventy feet and can live for three hundred years. They have the ability to withstand low rainfall or drought by reaching down hundreds of feet with their taproots into water basins beneath the desert. Not only can they survive, but they provide a home for woodpeckers, owls, and wrens and food for lizards, bats, and mammals, including man.*

The closer Brio got to Tucson, the larger the saguaros were. Brio remembered being awed by these giants as a young teacher in Tucson, and she was still amazed. From Tucson, she continued on I-10 East through a mountain wilderness terrain. It was late in the day when she reached Willcox, Arizona, where she stayed for the night.

The next morning, she journeyed through Eastern Arizona and Western Texas, which she found geologically interesting. The landscape included outcroppings of flat-topped bluffs, large, wide mesas, tall buttes, some cap-rocked, and hoodoos shaped like tents, chimneys, or pyramids. Between the rock outcroppings were plateaus with desert shrubs and small trees. Las Cruces, New Mexico was especially beautiful with the Organ Mountains rising to 3,900 feet. High desert terrain led to the Franklin Mountains, with El Paso, Texas at its base. As she stopped there for the night, she witnessed a brilliant sunset, typical of those she had nightly experienced when she had lived in Tucson.

As she left El Paso the next morning, she continued on Highway I-80 East through the Sierra Mountain range and the Apache range to Fort Stockton. (Until 1886, Fort Stockton had been an army fort, built to protect the pioneers from the Comanche Indians.) At Kerrville, the heart of the Hill Country in Texas, she returned to green territory, where vineyards and wineries had been established in the rolling hills. Only a short drive to San Antonio remained.

In San Antonio, Brio went directly to the condo to get her mail and to see how her residence had fared during her absence. In the living room, the baby grand and the television remained; the closet in the master bedroom contained her clothing; in the workroom were her computer desk and chair, a leather chair and ottoman, an end table and a standing lamp; in the guest bedroom, the four-poster bed remained. She looked under the bed and found the paintings and pictures that Richie and Hannah had put there. They had moved the mirrors, larger paintings, lamps, and the few remaining Persian carpets into the closets. In the garage, Brio found the furniture they had carried there and four filing cabinets, containing papers and records.

Hannah had hidden all traces of Brio's decoration and had "staged" the condo to her liking. The warmth of a colorful carpet had been replaced with a cold, white shag rug. The lovely aqua bedspread on the four-poster had been exchanged for a white-on-white comforter. The seascape, that had been hung above the bed, now resided in the closet. With the exception of one large oil painting on the living room fireplace, the walls of the condo were now bare and had been painted white. Hannah had turned the beauty and warmth that Brio had created into a cold, sterile atmosphere. Brio was happy to leave the condo and escape to a motel, where an attempt had been made to create a warm atmosphere away from home.

During the next week, Brio followed the plan she had devised. She spent most of her time working from her motel room. By the end of the week, Hannah had not come to show the condo to a prospective buyer nor had any other realtor. (No calling cards had been left on counters to indicate that they had been there.) Brio called Hannah's broker to complain about her neglect. Brio had listed the condo in early July. Although the housing market had been good during the summer, Hannah had failed to put the condo on multiple listing, keeping it unavailable to other realtors. As Brio started her journey home, she had mixed feelings. She was relieved that her own plans had been successful. She would now be able to live with a few treasures about her. But she was worried because she could not afford to keep the condo on the market much longer.

One final push of effort was needed to get her home, but her body and mind felt exhausted. Getting into California from the eastern border would be tedious and stressful. A traveler has to traverse two barriers into the state: the mountains and the deserts. Another problem would be the traffic. She chose the northern route from Arizona into California because the southern route would take her close to the heavy Los Angeles traffic.

To save money, she had to get home fast. She knew the major east/west highways to take, and she would rely upon her GPS for the north/south ones. She took I-West through Kerrville and Amarillo to Santa Rosa in New Mexico. As she traveled towards Albuquerque, she was tempted at Clines Corner to take a side trip to Santa Fe to revisit friends, her old home, and Holy Faith Church. Common sense encouraged her not to revisit at this time. She continued on 40 West to Gallup, New Mexico and across Arizona to Flagstaff. She hadn't revisited the magnificent Grand Canyon since Ben died, but she resisted the temptation to take the road there. So, from Flagstaff, she took 40 North across the border and into Barstow, California. Crossing the Mojave Desert was not as bleak as she remembered it. Towards the end, the beautiful Tehachapi Mountains welcomed her out of the desert. A final sprint from Bakersfield on 99 North brought her full circle back to Manteca.

When Brio stopped in the driveway of Lily's and Sam's house, she looked at her odometer. She had traveled 7,000 miles throughout the summer and fall. She had made four major trips:

1.   from Texas through OK, KS, and NE to Omaha

2. from NE through WY, UT, NV to CA

3. from CA through AZ, NM, to TX

4. from TX through NM, AZ, NV to CA

No wonder she felt exhausted! She had slept in twenty different motel beds. No wonder she felt homeless!

As she settled down for sleep that night, she remembered to thank God for her safety throughout the journeys and for the beauty and grandeur that had uplifted her along the way. She had had so many opportunities to appreciate God's creation, from the stark flat desert to the canyons, rocky buttes and mesas, leading to the rolling hills of the high plateaus and the foothills of the mountains. At each elevation, life of some sort had been sustained. (The giant saguaros were proof of that.) Her trips had been long, arduous, and often filled with tension, but she had been given an opportunity to experience the greatness of the United States and the majesty of God's creation.

Chapter XIX

Wounded

Brio had arrived back in California, but she could not move into her apartment in Stockton. Her furniture and other belongings were still in San Antonio. They had been taken by the moving company to a temporary storage unit until the van was filled with goods from three other households, a necessity for the moving company to make a profit. When they arrived two weeks later, Sam helped her to arrange the furniture in her apartment and then returned on the weekend to hang the paintings and a Nain rug on her walls. The paintings included a seascape, a scene of the Carmel Valley, a waterfront scene from the San Francisco area, and a street scene of Nob Hill. Pictures of her father, mother, husband, and daughter evoked memories of happier times.

During October and November, Sam helped Brio to put pressure on Hannah to get the condo sold. When escrow closed a few days before Thanksgiving, Brio received a cashier's check for the proceeds after the mortgage company and real estate amounts had been deducted. The amount was a pittance compared to the price that Brio had paid for the condo. However, she no longer had the expenses of a monthly mortgage payment, HOA fees, or utilities on the condo. She had lost her large *nest egg*, but she still had a tiny *nest*.

On Thanksgiving Day, Richie called Brio. It had been three months and she felt safe to answer.

"Hello."

"Thanks for answering, Brio. How are you?"

"I'm fine. I'm just surprised that you called."

"I haven't been well since you left, Brio."

"Oh? Sorry."

"Everything fell apart after you left. I was in a psychiatric hospital for a month."

"I told you that you needed counseling, Richie."

"You were right. I gave up hope and tried to commit suicide; I was taken to the hospital where I was kept for a month."

"Did they help you to get better?"

"Yes. At first, they had to get me physically well – get me to eat, wash myself, and sleep. I had a good nurse, like you were to me. Remember? When I was talking again, I had sessions with the psychiatrist. I'm not the same person, Brio." He paused. "I sent messages to you through Hannah, but you didn't answer, Brio."

"I never got them, Richie."

"Oh." He was silent.

"I'm listening now, Richie."

"I wanted to explain to you how I felt that night when you didn't come back."

"I'm listening." Brio waited for his explanation.

He continued: "I was excited and made preparations for your homecoming. I bought flowers and put them into a vase. I set the table and prepared the barbeque sauce. I had steaks ready to grill and vegetables for salad, which I washed and left to cut up so that they wouldn't get wilted. I had purchased a good red wine and a heart-shaped cake for dessert. Then I sat down to wait, hour after hour, and you didn't come. I expected to receive a call from you that you had run into trouble on the road, but you didn't call. About three o'clock, I gave up waiting, and I went to bed, feeling worried and sick. The next day, I tried to get you and you didn't answer. I left you a message which you ignored. A week later, I left you messages which you again ignored. When I realized that you weren't coming back, I felt broken." Brio was quiet. *He still sounds broken,* she thought, *wounded, like Mickey was towards the end.*

"Brio?"

"Yes, I'm here. I'm sorry for you, Richie."

"Well, I'm on my way to recovery now. But I'm leaving for Switzerland on December 10th, and I'd like to see you before I go. We could meet in a public place in California, if you like."

"Give me a day to think about it," she answered.

Brio worked out what would be safe for her. She could drive to the airport in Sacramento so that she and Richie would have transportation. They could get separate rooms in a Hilton which is large enough to have a restaurant, an indoor lounge and a patio area, where they could visit.

Richie agreed to the arrangements and sent her his travel itinerary.

When Brio saw Richie descending the elevator at the airport with his black leather satchel (the one she had given him for their trip to Paris), he did not look like the "same person." Gone was his look of arrogance. He was attired in simple conservative trousers and dress shirt. His broad shoulders were even more prominent now that he was forty pounds lighter. His visage brightened when he saw Brio. He came forward quickly and hugged her. She was the first to speak.

"You look thinner and your hair is shorter."

"Yes. They shaved my head at the hospital. My hair is growing out again."

On the way to the hotel, Richie described his flight from San Antonio. There were still a lot of passengers traveling home from Thanksgiving visits. There had been several legs to his journey, but no cancellations and no rerouting. When they reached the hotel, they registered and then went to their separate rooms to unpack. For the first of their long talks, they met at the pool, where they could lounge and Richie could smoke. Brio encouraged him to describe his life during the past three months.

"For several months after you left, I sat by the pool, drinking night and day. I let everything go in the house and garden, even the cats. The house was an absolute mess! My business problems got worse. I wasn't working. Bills were mounting up. Then Alfie took advantage of my condition. You remember Alfie?"

"Yes. He picked me up at the airport when I came back from California. What did he do?"

"He stole the customers from My Computer Technology. Jake and Alice were in on it. My three main employees turned against me!"

"What have you done about that, Richie?"

"So far, not much. The money is gone. I have a lawyer who is taking steps to close up the company."

"What about B and R Home Services? Has that house on King Road been finished?"

"Not yet. No money is left to complete it."

"Let's get back to the story of your depression, Richie."

"O.K. I had no one to turn to for help, no business employees I could trust, no family or friends. I decided the best way out was suicide, to shoot myself."

"Didn't you worry about what would happen to Maya and Basha?"

"I wasn't thinking clearly. All that I could think about was which gun to use and where I would do it." He paused.

"I'm listening."

"I took the gun that is designed to kill rather than to maim. I drove to the spot with the highest elevation of the highway, where you get the best view of San Antonio."

"I remember you took me there once. You used to like to go there." He nodded.

"I pulled over next to the railing, got out of the car, and stared at San Antonio below. When I got back into the car, I pointed the gun at my heart and pulled the trigger. The next thing I remember is waking up in the hospital."

"So, you were taken there by someone?"

"Yes. I saw the police report later. A motorist had stopped on the shoulder of the road, had seen me slumped over the steering wheel, and called 911."

"So, why were you still alive?"

"I don't know. The bullet didn't enter my heart and it didn't explode. Was it a miracle or a faulty bullet?" Brio shook her head.

"So, your wound was not large."

"No, not to my body, but I had a wounded spirit – I still do."

"Did the psychiatrist help you to understand why you attempted suicide?"

"Yes. We talked about my feelings of hopelessness and guilt and my inability to cope with my business problems and losses."

"Are you in a therapy program?"

"Yes, that's why I am here, to try to make amends, Brio."

"O.K. Let's rest for a while before dinner and then have another talk afterward."

After dinner, Richie showed Brio a five-page agreement document that he had on his I-pad. It had been drawn up by his lawyer. As they studied it together, Richie pointed out five proposals that would benefit Brio, and some which would benefit them both:

1. Richie would continue to make monthly payments to Brio until the private loan for his house was paid off or until either party was deceased.

2. Richie would pay Brio $50,000 when the King Road property sold.

3. Richie would make monthly payments on the Wells Fargo truck loan; he would become the sole owner of the vehicle at the end of the loan.

4. Richie would gradually reimburse Brio for her lost investment in B and R Home Services and My Security Services.

5. Richie would pay lawyer's fees for closing down B and R Home Services and My Computer Technology and would pay the lawyer's fees in the lawsuit: Nuborg Company vs. B and R Home Services and My Security Services, with Richie Campianno and Brioletta Martin as defendants.

Richie informed Brio that they would need to sign the documents before a notary, who would record them. Brio made notes on the five proposals and then said, "I'll think about this tonight and give you my answer in the morning."

After breakfast the following morning, Brio and Richie again sat by the pool. Brio analyzed each of the proposals, talking directly and forthrightly to Richie.

"Proposal #1 benefits each of us. The monthly income will help me to live a more comfortable life, and you will eventually own the house.

Proposal #2 will give me money in the bank for a rainy day.

Proposal #3 will eliminate one of my major monthly expenses; in the end, you will own the truck.

Proposal #4 will benefit me financially. I can gradually rebuild my *nest egg* and you can ease your conscience about my losses.

Proposal #5 is questionable. If you paid the lawyer's fees, it would be beneficial to me. However, we could both be losers if the lawsuit goes against us."

"I agree with all of your points, Brio, but will you sign the agreement?" Richie asked.

"Yes. Let's go to see the notary. Then, how about an excursion into the Old West?"

"O.K. Do I need a horse?" he asked impishly

As Brio drove Richie to Nevada City in her Mini, she took Highway 80 East, showing him sights of Sacramento, leading to the foothills of the Sierra Nevada Mountains. At Auburn, she turned north onto Highway 49, named for the forty-niners of the Gold-Rush period. In Nevada City, she explained that the town had been named for the mountains, not for the state of Nevada. (The word, *nevada*, means *snow-covered* in Spanish). The little town was built on rolling hills, covered with tall redwoods. Brio drove through the historic downtown area, where she pointed out the National Hotel, the oldest operating hotel in California, the bell-towered firehouse with its Victorian "gingerbread" architecture, and the Nevada Theater, where Mark Twain gave lectures as The Humorist of the West.

After parking the car, Brio took Richie on a walkingtour of side streets, past old houses built in the 1800's and 1900's, all well-preserved. One wooden house, with an expansive veranda, had been turned into an elegant bed-and-breakfast, where Brio and Ben had frequently stayed. Following a hearty dinner in a restaurant pretending to be an Old West saloon, they returned to the Hilton in Sacramento. Before retiring for the night, they enjoyed a few drinks on the patio.

"Here's to you, Brio," toasted Richie, raising his glass.

"Here's to you, Richie. Stay well!"

Chapter XX
What about Richie?

In the following three months, Brio had eleven calls from Richie while he was in Switzerland:

Richie called to say that his flight had been long and tedious, but he had slept most of the way. Basha and Maya were with him in the cat carrier. Because Richie had registered them as support animals, they were allowed to be in the passenger area with him.

—⁊⁊— —⁊⁊— —⁊⁊—

He had found a one-bedroom fully-furnished apartment on the Rue Philippe Plantamour 6, 1201, in Geneva, Switzerland, not far from the United Nations building.

Richie called while waiting at a bus stop, across from the UN building. With his cell camera, he explained, he took a picture of the building, a beige-colored structure set back from the street. Leading up to it, the lawn is bordered by cedar trees and a row of flags of the different nations represented at the UN. (It was *just as Brio remembered it*).

—⁊⁊— —⁊⁊— —⁊⁊—

His work hours are from 7:30 a.m. until 3:30 p.m. There is a cafeteria for meals and croissants and coffee are available throughout the day. His job right now is to study and read books, pamphlets, and articles in preparation for later on-site work.

Richie called from his apartment to say that he is lonely. He misses Brio and San Antonio. He feels depressed and hopeless. He saw a doctor last week about giving him a fatal injection. In Switzerland, that is legal.

(Richie was sobbing when he ended the call.)

—⁂— —⁂— —⁂—

Richie called from Lyon, France. He took Brio's advice and escaped from his apartment for the weekend. He got a loaner car from the UN, which he will be allowed to keep until he is given a permanent company car. He left the city of Geneva and drove through the countryside and across the border into France. The scenery was pretty and similar to the drive from Paris to Provins.

—⁂— —⁂— —⁂—

Richie called with news about San Antonio. He had given Karen, his only remaining employee, the job of dealing with Brio's belongings. Karen called an auction house to collect the rugs and furniture that they thought would sell. Brio's furniture from Richie's living room was moved into the garage. Boxes of family pictures and personal papers are on their way to Brio via UPS.

—⁂— —⁂— —⁂—

Richie called with good and bad news. He had finally gotten paid. He was happy to send Brio two payments for his house loan. Unfortunately, he injured his ankle in the garage, while trying to deal with his loaner car, which is a "piece of shit." The car has been taken back by the UN. He was taken to the hospital, where they put a pin in his ankle and set it in plaster, which will have to stay on for six or more weeks.

—⚬— —⚬— —⚬—

His supervisor at the UN has been critical, but he has allowed him to work from home.

Richie called about the house on King Road in San Antonio. The realtor has not been able to sell the house because the renovation was so poorly done; the floors were uneven; the trim was not neatly joined; the cabinets were shoddy.

—⚬— —⚬— —⚬—

Richie has found a company that buys and sells houses needing work. They will buy the King Road property for $250,000. (*Richie asked Brio to claim that she has occupied the King house for* six *months. Brio refused to lie about her residency.*)

Richie called again about King. He has found a company that will give him a mortgage of $100,000 on the property. Because of his poor credit rating, the mortgage would have to be made by Brio. On paper, she would be making the payments, but actually he would make them through her. (*Brio did not want to get saddled with another mortgage and refused.*)

—⁂— —⁂— —⁂—

Richie called about the abuse charge made in August, which was hanging over his head. Would Brio contact the district attorney's office and drop the charge?

(*When Brio called the office, she received a message that the case is awaiting indictment.*)

—⁂— —⁂— —⁂—

Richie called with good news. He had gotten his second check from the UN, and he is sending Brio the house loan payment. Karen had finally sent him Brio's Christmas gift of inspirational quote cards. He has been reading one each day and thinking about it.

—⁂— —⁂— —⁂—

Richie called and said that he hadn't called for some time because he has been feeling anxious and depressed. When he can walk again, he will have to go back to the office at the UN to do his work there. He dislikes Switzerland and the Swiss people. He feels trapped in Geneva. He would like to live in France, but even if he had a car, commuting might not be possible. He is escaping with alcohol. If God is punishing him, he is certainly doing a good job of it!

—⁂— —⁂— —⁂—

In the next three months, Brio received calls from Richie less and less frequently. She was relieved that he was no longer turning to her with his financial or emotional problems. Although she still cared about him, she felt that he needed professional help.

Richie had often talked about his formative years in the Mideast. Attempting to better understand him, Brio studied the history of Syria, Lebanon, and Israel:

After World War I, the League of Nations divided Greater Syria, which had been under French control, into the countries of Lebanon and Syria. Lebanon was bordered by the Mediterranean Sea on its west, Israel on its south, and Syria on its east and north.

From the beginning of the two nations, there were conflicts between Israel and its bordering Arab neighbors. In Lebanon, a brutal, bloody civil war broke out between the Christian Right, conservative Muslims and the Palestinian, left-leaning Muslims.

Syria had a six-day war with Israel, ending with Israel taking the Golan Heights from Syria. Then the Syrians intervened in the civil war in Lebanon. Because of their stronger military force, they occupied Lebanon for twenty-nine years. The occupation finally ended after the Cedar Revolution in 2005.

Richie's mother was Lebanese; she had experienced its history. Through her, Richie learned about the bloody civil war, when brother fought against brother. When the Syrians captured his family and took them to Syria, Richie lived from ages four through twelve in fear of his life. To protect himself and his brothers, Richie fought vicious Syrian gangs in the street.

Brio thought that Richie was still "fighting gangs in the street." He had described to her that period of his life more than once. However, she wondered if he would ever be able to leave his ego-centered, troubled world.

Chapter XXI

Confused

In mid-March, Richie again contacted Brio. He had been unable to endure his loneliness and unhappiness in living abroad. He is, therefore, returning to San Antonio where he will stay in the house that he purchased with a loan from Brio. He will find work ASAP and will continue to make payments on the house loan.

A week later, he called from San Antonio. He feels overwhelmed. The house, pool, and garden are in a sad state. He is out of money and can barely pay for living expenses. April 1, 2023 is the date that has been set for the hearing in the district court. His lawyer recently filed a motion to withdraw from the case. He has found a new lawyer, but she does not have enough time to prepare for the hearing. Richie will have to represent himself and will need Brio's help. Because Brio has been made a defendant in the case, she will be liable for a default judgment if she ignores the court procedure. He is sending her material to bring her up-to-date on their case.

On March 23rd, Richie sent Brio sixty-seven pages of court documents and files, including a State of Texas certificate of formation of B and R Home Services;

the construction contract; the company operating agreement; the plaintiff's original petition and the amended petition; the defendant's original answer and the amended answer; Richie's affidavit; a certificate of non-appearance of Richie; a motion to quash the depositions of Richie and Brio; three separate motions for withdrawal of counsel for the defendants. In addition, Richie sent: twelve scans of xerox copies, including a proof of insurance; a profit and loss statement for 2021; a payroll statement for October, 2021 to January, 2022; a balance sheet for January, 2022. (The range of the dates for the documents was from December, 2020 through March, 2023.)

After Brio had read all of the material, her head was reeling. There was too much to digest in such a short time. She had no time to consult a lawyer for herself and no money with which to pay one. So, she consulted a trusted friend, who advised her to remain passive for the time being. However, Brio believed in the old adage, "God helps those who help themselves." She felt that burying her head in the sand was too dangerous. Doing *nothing* to resolve the issue would achieve *nothing*. She decided that she would attend the hearing to gather information and to avoid a charge of non-appearance in court. She made reservations for a flight to Austin, Texas and a hotel room near the district court. She needed to be at the Sacramento Airport by 4:00 a.m. on April 1st. Late on the night of March 31st, Richie called to say that the hearing had been postponed until May.

A month later, Richie informed Brio that the date of the hearing was set for May 19th. The new lawyer he has hired will be ready to represent B and R Home Services, My Computer Technology, and Richie and Brio as defendants. Brio need not attend the hearing because she was only an investor, a silent partner in the business.

Brio waited anxiously for the results of the hearing. In the afternoon of the second day in court, Richie called to report that the hearing was over. The judge exonerated Brio, but found Richie guilty. Nuborg and Company, LLC, was awarded $1,200,000, and Richie was given only thirty days to appeal.

"Are you going to appeal?" asked Brio.

"I can't," he answered. "I can't add more lawyer's fees to my huge debt."

"I'm happy for myself, but concerned for you," Brio responded. "Will you be left with anything?"

"Only my residence, because it has a lien on it, and one of my vehicles for transportation. Nuborg will get the house on King Road, and they will be able to garnish my wages and take any other income I can make."

"How do you feel?" she asked.

"Angry. Their lawyer tore me apart. He painted me as a heartless, pathetic individual."

Brio responded, "Lawyers are not trained to be merciful." She paused. "What will you do now, Richie?"

"Who knows?"

"You'll work it out," she responded, encouragingly.

When the phone call was over, Brio began to think about herself. She felt relieved. She could now go to sleep at night without worrying what might happen the next day. She was exhausted from living in Richie's world, a world full of uncertainty and deception. She now had an opportunity to once again live among people with like values: a belief in God and Christian mores, and an attempt to follow God's commandments, to "love Him with one's heart and soul and to love one's neighbor as oneself."

In the summer days following the court judgement, Brio began taking walks along the lake near her residence, to begin to heal her mind and spirit. The lake was bordered by lovely, expensive homes, similar to ones that she and Ben had owned. Towards the end of the walk, she sat down on a bench to watch the activity on and near the lake. There were no boaters on the lake and only an occasional pedestrian on the path. Brio heard a splash in the water. As she watched a duck going "bottom up" for a fish, she briefly thanked God for the duck and the fish and for the jewels of sunlight on the shimmering lake.

Brio's cell phone chirped. It was Richie. He was calling to tell her that his finances were beginning to be handled.

He did not go into details, but he assured Brio that he would again make his monthly house payments. Every four to six weeks, he continued to call, to inform her about his life: the jobs he was able to find; the state of the house and garden; the health of Basha, Maya, and himself; and his loneliness as a bachelor. He always ended the call with regrets that she was no longer with him.

Brio listened with mixed feelings. His tone and words reminded her of times when he had been caring and thoughtful. However, he had been a chameleon, and she was concerned that he still had power of attorney over her; so, she found a local lawyer who removed Richie's power, giving Brio legal control of herself.

Chapter XXII

The Healing of Brio

A year later, Brio moved from her studio apartment in an assisted living building to a two-bedroom apartment in a gated community. When she returned to California after her abuse in Texas, her family felt that she needed the emotional help and care which she would receive in assisted living. At first, Brio felt safe, but as she began to heal from her abuse, she felt confined in her small studio room and out-of-place in a home where she was daily among residents who were physically and/or mentally compromised. Furthermore, living again on her own would be $1,000 less expensive per month, and it would allow her the freedom to pursue a more active lifestyle.

Brio spent several months looking for an apartment. During this time, Richie frequently called to convince her to return to San Antonio to live with him. He described how he had changed his life for the better: he was working steadily again as a computer technician; he was taking good care of the house and garden; he was regularly attending church; the minister was encouraging him to mend the relationship with his "wife."

Brio's response was to advise Richie to wait for a year to see if he was capable of a long-term change. By October, Brio had found a two-bedroom apartment in a large gated community. Her apartment was the end one of a three-apartment bungalow. The front faced the street, and the side faced an enclosed patio area. The rental came with a garage for her car, locked gates on the property, and a keyed mailbox. Within the gates were well-manicured lawns, walkways, majestic redwood trees, and a swimming pool and exercise room.

Since she had sold most of her furniture in Texas, she needed living room and kitchen furniture. She purchased a couch, a loveseat, a coffee table, and end tables for the living room and a table with four chairs for the kitchen. She already had a four-poster bed and nightstands for the master bedroom and a computer desk and leather chair with ottoman for the second bedroom, which became a workroom.

Not long after moving in, she began to convert the patio area into a garden. Along the fences, she planted honeysuckle vines. In wooden planter boxes, she planted a rose bush, a camellia bush, two Queen palms, and a variety of colorful flowers. When finished, she had a private place to relax and meditate outdoors and a spacious area indoors for reading, writing, listening to music, watching T.V., and working at the computer.

To make her "nest egg" complete, she purchased a used Wurlitzer baby grand piano, which was in good condition. At the assisted living home, she had been able to play the piano only at certain times, and never privately so that she could practice scales or arpeggios, which the residents did not want to listen to. On her own piano, she could play at any time of the day or night. Shortly after her purchase, the church that she had been attending needed an organist. She was happy to accept the position because she could now practice and prepare the music at home as well as at church. The organist position was a blessing to her; she not only enjoyed being active in music again; it provided an additional income for her.

Little by little, Brio was able to rebuild her life. A year later, Richie was still in touch with her. For her birthday in August, he sent a computer picture of a sweet little boy holding his hands in the shape of a heart. A message accompanied it: "Happy Birthday! I am immensely grateful to have you in my life. Thank you for everything you have done. As we celebrate your special day and another year of your life, I wish you joy and happiness.!"

In September, Brio sent Richie a birthday message, wishing him happiness. The next communication from him was on October 14, 2024. It was a picture of a closet area, showing a 350-pound server that had fallen on top of a ladder. The second picture was of Richie, lying with eyes closed, on a hospital examination table. Richie included a message: "I am so sorry. I have been in an accident. The server fell on my head and shoulder. I don't know how it didn't kill me. I am going through all kinds of treatments."

Brio sent him a message of condolence and concern for his health. Richie did not respond verbally, but he sent $600 from his bank account as his monthly house payment. (It was supposedly all he could afford.) Brio did not hear from him again. Christmas came and went, and the New Year began. This was perhaps a blessing for Brio. She was no longer subject to his behavior or influenced by his words or tone of voice. During the next eleven months, she thought of him less and less. Finally, her mind stopped wavering between thoughts of abuse and fear or caring and safety.

Chapter XXIII

Seeking Justice

On a sunny day in November, Brio began her morning walk at the complex. She strolled between the two giant redwoods at the corner of her bungalow and past the swimming pool. The winding pathway took her past other bungalows facing the street, around a corner, past private patio areas, and around a large swath of lawn area, which led to the mailboxes.

When she opened her mailbox with her key, she found a large envelope. She was happy; she had been expecting a publisher to send her a "galley" copy of her new book. However, when she got home and opened it, she found a legal document: the arbitration lawsuit case of Samuel Spanner v. Richie Campianno, My Computer Technology LLC, B and R Home Services LLC, and Brioletta Martin. Brio's heart sank.

She sat down and studied the document. Spanner's claim was that on 3-22-23, he had entered into a contract withB and R Home Services LLC for the construction of a pool and cabana. The contract had been signed by Brio as Director and Shareholder of the company. The complaint charged breach of contract and fraud.

Brio's first reaction was shock. However, upon further studying the complaint, she saw the discrepancy in dates. The contract was dated 3-22-23, but Brio had been physically abused by Richie on 8-15-22 and had immediately left Texas, driving first to Omaha, Nebraska and then to California, where she took up residence. Seven months had elapsed since Richie's company had begun the construction project. Brio determined that her name had been illegally signed; so, she could not be held responsible.

Looking for other illegalities, she read the document a third time. She saw that on 2-23-24, the corporate privileges for B and R Home Services LLC were forfeited by the Comptroller of Texas for failure to file reports and to pay franchise taxes. Since Richie's companies had been terminated, there were no company funds to be gained from a lawsuit, but Texas law held that shareholders/owners could be held responsible if they had monetarily gained from fraudulent practices. Thus, both Richie and Brio were liable for all debts occurred during the forfeiture period.

I wish I had never invested in B and R, Brio thought. It has been a millstone around my neck! In an attempt to see if she had missed something else important, she studied the court document again. She found a false statement that Richie had made to the opposing lawyer: "I sold my ownership interest to Brioletta Martin on 11-16-22. We signed the paperwork before a notary in Sacramento, CA." A light suddenly flashed into Brio's mind, concerning the Thanksgiving weekend she had spent with Richie that November.

After three months of no communication, he had begged to see her. When they met, he told her that he had been in a psychiatric hospital for several months. His therapist had helped him to analyze his thoughts and actions that led to his attempted suicide. She had advised changes to his lifestyle, and he was "turning over a new leaf" by trying to make amends to Brio for her financial losses.

He had had his lawyer draw up a plan with five proposals for reimbursing her. Brioremembered the proposals and the occasion that they had read them together by the pool at the hotel. They were on his I-pad; Brio was not given a printed copy, but she had recorded the five listings. She agreed with the proposals, including his promise to continue his home loan payments to her.

When Richie left to return to San Antonio, he promised to send a printed copy of the document to Brio so that she could thoroughly study "the fine print." He never sent it. He continued his monthly house payments until an injury occurred when he was installing a heavy computer server. Then all communication ceased.

Now Brio understood that the Thanksgiving weekend, when the document was presented to her, had been a ploy to establish her as the sole owner of B and R Services, making her responsible for the business contracts and the debts incurred. Once again, Richie had used and manipulated her. It had been a clever act of deceit, rather than a congenial, pleasant time together.

Brio decided to study the court document again to see if there were other clues of Richie's deceit. She found that she had overlooked Richie's change of address from San Antonio to Dallas, where his younger brother lived. She wondered if Richie had sold his house while still owing her 90% of the repayment plan. When she searched public records for present and past owners of the property, the records showed that Richie had purchased the property on 10-16-20, the date on which Brio had withdrawn money from her bank account.

Richie had owned the house from October, 2020 through March,2022, a time period when Richie and Brio were still together. At that time, the lawsuit with Nuborg and Company was pending. Brio left Richie in August, 2022, but the trial did not occur until May, 2023. When Brio asked Richie if Nuborg would be awarded his house as part of the judgement against him, Richie answered that they could not take it because it had a lien on it.

Public records proved that Richie had lied to her. Richie had sold his house to his brother **before** the trial judgement. His brother kept the house only until March, 2024, when it became the property of Richie's ex-wife. It had subsequently been put into an irrevocable trust in her family's name.

Brio finally realized the extent of Richie's greed, selfishness, and lack of mercy. She remembered her niece Maggie saying, "Richie is an evil man! Don't trust him! Take care for your life, Aunt Brio!" At the time, Brio thought that she could help Richie to become a better man. But his pattern of immorality was too firmly entrenched. *A tree is incapable of producing new leaves if it is rotten from within.*

Brio knew that she had flaws, but determination was not one of them. All she needed was a little support to go forward. She would search for a good, honest Texas lawyer, and she would trust in God to help her, as he had so often done in the past. She was **determined** to handle it "one day at a time," praying for justice to prevail.

THE END

www.ingramcontent.com/pod-product-compliance
Lightning Source LLC
Chambersburg PA
CBHW020537160726
47991CB00002B/474